Caring
and curing

A philosophy of
medicine and social work

Caring and curing

A philosophy of
medicine and social work

R.S. Downie
and
Elizabeth Telfer

METHUEN
LONDON AND NEW YORK

First published in 1980 by
Methuen & Co. Ltd
11 New Fetter Lane, London EC4P 4EE
Published in the USA by
Methuen & Co.
in association with Methuen, Inc.
733 Third Avenue, New York, NY 10017
© *1980 R.S. Downie & Elizabeth Telfer*
Typeset by Red Lion Setters, Holborn, London
Printed in Great Britain at the
University Press, Cambridge

British Library Cataloguing in Publication Data

Downie, Robert Silcock
Caring and curing.
1. Social service – Philosophy
2. Medicine – Philosophy
I. Title   II. Telfer, Elizabeth
361'.001   HV31   80-40246

ISBN 0-416-71800-0
ISBN 0-416-71810-8 Pbk

Contents

Acknowledgements

Our debts philosophical and practical are many: to students and teachers of medicine and social work with whom we have discussed the issues; to the Working Party on 'Values' of the Central Council for Education and Training in Social Work; to the S.S.R.C. Seminar Group on Philosophy and Welfare led by Professor Noel Timms; to the Editor of the *Journal of Medical Ethics* for permission to use material by the authors previously printed in the Journal; to John Naylor of Methuen for encouraging us to think that this would be a worthwhile project; to our secretaries, Anne Valentine and Wilma White, for making sense of our handwriting. We gratefully acknowledge influence, advice and assistance from all these quarters, and also from the thirteenth fairy we have undoubtedly forgotten to mention.

R.S.D.
E.T.

Preface

This book is intended for those engaged in medicine, social work and related occupations, or the 'caring professions'. Its aims are to be an introduction to philosophy specially designed for the caring professions, and at the same time to be a philosophy of the caring professions. These two aims are linked, in that the best way to introduce philosophy is not to talk about it but to engage in it, to philosophize; and the most exciting way to philosophize is to offer a reasoned but controversial point of view on matters to which people are professionally committed or about which they feel strongly. In other words, to make the activity of philosophizing seem exciting and worthwhile it is essential to formulate a philosophy.

Our philosophy of the caring professions has two main features. First, we shall argue for the essential unity of the caring professions. It is traditional for medically related professions to see themselves as concerned with health in all its aspects, and for social-work-related professions to see themselves as concerned with welfare. Our view is that the two concepts of health and welfare are different aspects of a single value judgment as to what sort of life a person ought to be enabled to live in his society. Assuming the validity of this position we shall place the concepts of health and welfare in the context of a philosophy of the natural and social sciences, and of a moral and political philosophy. Finally, we shall develop a total metaphysical view of the meaning of human life in the whole scheme of things. In other words, in expounding our view of the essential unity of the caring professions we shall introduce the main branches of philosophy: the theory of knowledge and the philosophy of science and social science; moral and political philosophy; metaphysics.

The other main feature of the philosophy we offer is our attempt to show the limits of scientific expertise in relation to human behaviour. Here we shall be concerned both with the impossibility (as we shall argue) of complete scientific explanation of human action, and therefore the desirability of supplementing the scientific education of medical and social workers with some broader humane disciplines; and also with the impossibility of a science of values, and therefore the desirability of including within the education of medical and social workers some training in the conceptual skills which will help them to cope with the pressing problems of morality (or 'ethics' as they are often called in medicine and social work). In investigating the nature of values, value judgments and so on we shall discuss many of the current moral dilemmas in medicine and social work. We can therefore claim that this book is both an introduction to philosophy and an application of it to many of the problems of the caring professions.

University of Glasgow   R.S. Downie
October 1979   Elizabeth Telfer

Introduction:
The relevance of
philosophy to medicine
and social work

Why should a doctor or a social worker take time off from a busy life to consider what philosophers might say about their activities? Is there a place for philosophy or 'ethics' in the curriculum of a medical student, a nurse or a social worker? Had these questions been raised twenty years ago the answers might have been discouraging, for medical practitioners and social workers at that time saw little reason to consider subjects other than a narrow range of natural and social sciences. Moreover, if they had turned to the writings of contemporary philosophers they would have found little to encourage a professional interest, for philosophy tended then to be an inward-looking subject, much concerned with its own methodology and the purifying of itself from anything empirical or evaluative, and thought to have no bearing on substantive moral or political questions. Small wonder, then, that there was no incentive for the medical man to make room for philosophy alongside his biochemistry or the social worker to make room for philosophy alongside his psychology or sociology.

In contrast with this period, the danger at the present time is that there is too *much* enthusiasm for philosophy on the part of the caring professions. More precisely, the danger is that the

nature of philosophy has been misunderstood, in that it is sometimes considered to be another expertise which could be put
alongside biochemistry or psychology, and so to have a practical
relevance to medicine or social work which it does not and cannot
have. This false view of philosophy has arisen partly out of a
development of what are called the 'ethics' of the professions.
Take first medicine.

The medical and nursing professions have always had a code of
ethics, by which is meant general rules governing professional
conduct. These consist partly of approved aims and methods,
such as might be found in the Hippocratic Oath, and partly of
more specific prohibitions as are laid down from time to time by
bodies such as the British Medical Association, the General
Nursing Council, the British Association of Social Workers, and
their equivalents in other countries. For example, it is regarded as
'unethical' to advertise one's professional services or to try to
poach patients from other practitioners. More recently, however,
due to developments within medicine and changes in public
morality, there have grown up for nurses and doctors a set of
problems which they would regard as 'ethical', but for which
there are no obvious guidelines laid down in existing codes of
ethics. For example, due to improvements in care it is possible to
keep patients who would formerly have died 'alive' in some sense
of that term. Their brains are 'dead' but the rest of their body is
maintained alive with the help of costly machinery. It becomes
an ethical question to decide at what point this machinery
should be switched off. But ethical questions of this kind are not
covered by the traditional code, and public opinion in any case no
longer rests content with traditional medical answers to such
questions. The medical profession therefore looks for help in discussing these issues, and one obvious direction in which to turn is
to that sphere in which ethics is professionally practised – to the
philosophers. This is well and good, except that philosophical
ethics does not provide the degree of precision and practical guidance which is to be found in traditional medical ethics.

Problems of a different sort arise in social work, but they too
lead to the creation of false expectations about philosophy. Over
the past ten years social workers have had what might be termed a
crisis of identity. Moving from older ideas of the social worker as
a philanthropist or friend, through psychoanalytical models of

the social worker/client relationship, social workers have more recently been depicted as agents both of social change and of social control, and with these problems of identity have come associated problems of the ethics of political intervention, of confidentiality, of paternalism, and more generally of the whole system of values on which social work is built. Problems of this kind are very much philosophical problems, but the sort of help which can be obtained from philosophical discussion needs careful qualification. What then is the relationship between philosophical theory and medical or social work practice? To put the question in another way, what is the *relevance* of philosophy to the caring professions?

This question is really a specific form of the general question of the relationship between moral philosophy and actual conduct, and there is no easy or widely agreed answer to it, because philosophers have seen this relationship in different ways in different historical periods. One important contemporary view, however, is that the philosopher should be concerned with the logical analysis of the concepts and principles of moral discourse. An objection is sometimes made to conceptual analysis that it gives us no guidance on questions of moral substance. But to have a grasp of the complexities of moral concepts and principles is clearly of great assistance in the forming of one's own moral point of view. For example, medical and social workers are sometimes criticized for being too authoritarian in their dealings with patients or clients, and they sometimes reply that they have a right to be authoritarian since they are experts or authorities in their subjects and therefore know what is best for their patients or clients. Conceptual analysis would be of assistance here in clarifying the ambiguities in terms such as 'authority', 'authoritarian', 'authoritative', and indeed 'rights'. In this book we shall make use of the techniques of linguistic or conceptual analysis with the aim of clarifying and showing the relationships between concepts such as 'health', 'welfare', 'equality', 'autonomy'. It is our belief that progress is not likely to be made in the current moral debates in medicine and social work unless those who are best qualified to conduct them – medical and social workers – acquire some skills in conceptual analysis, and our hope is that this book will demonstrate the usefulness of such skills. In this aspect of our book we shall no doubt be influenced by our own moral views but our aim here is not to recommend moral positions but to *clarify* concepts.

The defect of some contemporary moral philosophy is not that it is analytical, since analysis has always been a function of philosophy right back to Plato, but that it has recently tended to neglect its other function, of being synthetic or synoptic. The philosopher when performing this traditional function acts as the spectator of all time and all place. What this means is that he presents a total view of human nature and its place in the scheme of things. In other words, the great philosophers of the past did not depict human nature as if it were divided into the compartments of the physical, the mental, the social, the moral, the political, the economic, the aesthetic and so on, nor did they divide their inquiries with such a jealous regard for the identity of this or that specialism as we do, but rather they presented a total view of man, his society and the significance of his life. It is this synoptic vision which is the appeal of the great works of philosophy of the past. Plato's *Republic*, Aristotle's *Ethics*, Hobbes' *Leviathan*, Spinoza's *Ethics* all provide a *total* vision of man and society, and these visions are intellectually satisfying. They might indeed be said to appeal in the end to the *imagination* as much as to the intellect, in that they each have a characteristic synoptic vision of the world.

In this book we shall try to carry out the synthetic or synoptic function of philosophy. Thus we shall try to show the connections between the general principles and concepts of health and welfare and we shall relate each to their value bases. We shall then go on to sketch in the wider social and political context in which the practitioners of the principles of health and welfare carry out their activities, and to describe the kinds of knowledge which underlie those activities. Finally, we shall move to ultimate questions about the meaning of life, questions which must occur to all reflective medical and social workers as they deal with the tragedies of premature death, warped personality, and darkened minds, or the triumphs of pain bravely borne, handicap overcome and ordinary frustration patiently endured. By adopting this synoptic approach to knowledge and value we shall try to develop the idea of the unity of life. Inquiries of this grand and synoptic sort are inevitably pretentious, but the cure for inadequate philosophy is not *no philosophy*, but *better philosophy*.

The view of man which will emerge is that of a mind/body unity the actions of which are not susceptible to complete scientific explanation, even in principle. In other words, we reject determinism and materialism as philosophies of persons. The view of nature we present is that of 'things' and their processes completely explicable in material and deterministic terms, but of human purpose as creative and irreducible to causality. It is of course morally dangerous to say that 'persons' and 'things' are all that exist, because we are then tempted to ignore the categories of the non-human animal and the natural environment, with the likelihood of damage to these. But the types of explanation relevant to animal behaviour or vegetable growth are extensions, or contractions, of the explanations which apply paradigmatically to persons and things: the purposive and the causal. And these are the categories of explanation we shall mainly be concerned with in this book. From them, and using no other categories, we can derive an account of the meaning of life; philosophies of a transcendent purpose for life can be coherent, but in our view they are not necessary to give life meaning.

There are many objections to this undertaking which we shall discuss as we come to them. But there is one which should be mentioned at the outset since it concerns our qualifications to write the book. How can authors who are neither social workers nor medical practitioners write about topics which require knowledge and experience of both? The answer is, first, that insofar as we are attempting to provide instruction it is not in the principles of medicine or social work but in philosophy. The same difficulty after all can arise for a philosopher writing about science, theology, art, mathematics, etc., who is not himself qualified in the other discipline. In each case he must do the best he can and be ready to seek advice from those qualified in the other discipline. Second, we are not in any case attempting to provide instruction, but rather to suggest some ideas and theories which the practitioners of social work and medicine might be able to take up and develop in their own more specialized contexts. Third, although not *practitioners* of the caring professions, we are *consumers* of them and familiar with the views of other consumers. This gives us a viewpoint which the practitioner can usefully heed. These then are our defences for venturing into this important interdisciplinary area.

1 The value base of the caring professions

What are values?

The practice of medical and social work exemplifies or incorporates certain *values*, which we may regard as forming the *value-base* of medicine and social work. The sense of 'values' which is in question here, however, needs some examination. Presumably we are saying that *qua* doctor or *qua* social worker, and perhaps *qua* institutor or administrator of social work, a person necessarily has certain values. What is it for a person to have or possess values?[1]

To answer this question, we may consider first what kinds of thing are naturally spoken of as a person's values: we say, for example, 'My values (or 'my values in life') are integrity, kindness, beauty'. Does this just mean 'These are the things I value'? No, because I may value highly my sports car or my mink coat, but it would be odd to say that these things were among my *values*, except in jest.

This is not a *moral* point, about the triviality of having such things as one's values. Rather it is a conceptual point about the kinds of thing that can comprehensibly be said to be among a person's values. In the case of a sports car or a mink coat, we can always ask *why* someone sets such a high value on such things, and get an answer in terms of more general considerations. For example, a man may say he values his sports car because it gives him freedom or excitement, and a woman may value her mink coat because it looks beautiful. But where something is to be regarded as among a person's values, he has no further reason why these things are valued. If kindness is among a man's values then it is valued for its own sake, and other things (e.g. a thoughtful letter) can be valued as exemplifying the fundamental value.

Can we then say that a person's values are simply those things which he values *for their own sakes*? This is not very informative without further discussion of what it is to value something. Now a great deal has been written on this; but a fairly rough-and-ready characterization will do for our present purposes. We might try the approach that valuing is to do with preference and choice: to value something more highly than something else is to choose to have it or get it in preference to the other thing, to choose to hold onto it in preference to the other thing, and so on.

Described in this way, valuing is essentially *comparative*, whereas simply having certain values does not seem to be so. But we can accommodate the apparent non-comparativeness of what are said to be a person's values in terms of the comparative notion, by saying that a person's values are those things which for their own sakes he prefers to everything else. Thus, if beauty is among a person's values, he will, given a choice, sacrifice all other things in order to achieve beauty unless, of course, one of his other values is also at stake, or he is weakwilled and fails to do what he thinks he should.

But this account of valuing fails to distinguish between two distinct ways in which something might be valued for its own sake. The distinction is best explained by means of an example. Suppose a shy, reserved person takes a lot of pains to keep his doings to himself, sacrificing all sorts of possibilities in order to maintain this concealment, apparently with no further end in view; we would then say that privacy is one of his values. Now there are two possibilities: on the one hand, he may say that *he* likes privacy but is happy to let others be more extrovert and unbuttoned. On the other hand, he may *disapprove* of those who prattle about their affairs, and try to bring up his children to set the same store by privacy as he does himself. Again, a person who values thrift and enterprise for their own sakes may either simply *like* to be thrifty and enterprising, as a matter of temperament, or he may *approve* of thrift and enterprise in himself and others, be ashamed of himself if he is extravagant or unenterprising, and so on. We can call the first kind of values 'liking-values' (though *liking* will be too mild a word to convey the strength of some valuings of this kind) and the second kind 'ideal-values'. When people speak of values they more often mean ideal values, and if we use the word 'values' without qualification we shall be referring to ideal values.

Are ideal values the same as *moral* values? This all depends on what is meant by 'moral', which is a very slippery term indeed. Ideal values certainly possess some features which are usually thought of as characteristic of morality. For example, they affect conduct: a person's ideal values – his approvals – have a bearing on what he does. Of course a person does not *always* do what he approves of – in other words, he may on occasion be false to his ideal values – but if a man's alleged ideal value had *no* bearing on his conduct in practice we would say that it was not really one of his ideal values. Again, a man's ideal values, as distinct from his liking-values, have the *universal* quality which is characteristic of morality: we said that if a man has an ideal value he judges others as well as himself in terms of it. On the other hand, some ideal values which some people have – such as the cultivation of physical beauty – do not seem to have the right *subject-matter* for morality as traditionally conceived, which (it might be said) is to do with human happiness and misery, human welfare and so on.

It is really a matter of choice whether or not one calls such ideal values as the pursuit of physical beauty for its own sake *moral* values. If the subject matter of morality is narrowly conceived, for example as human happiness, then it may be that this particular ideal value cannot be regarded as a moral value. But if one speaks, more vaguely, of human *welfare* as the subject-matter of morality, then the pursuit of physical beauty, and indeed any other ideal value, takes its place as part of morality, since the person whose value it is may be said to conceive of the realization of this value as part of a proper life for a human being – in other words, as part of human welfare. The main kinds of value with which medicine and social work are concerned, to do with the relief of misery and the promotion of happiness, belong fairly uncontroversially to morality even in a narrow sense, but there might be some values connected with these pursuits which would fall outside a narrow definition of morality: if, for example, medicine is seen as having the promotion of physical beauty as one of its values.

We have spoken so far of values as *belonging* to people or groups of people: a value, according to our account so far, is something which is as a matter of fact valued in a particular way by someone or some group. Now some philosophers, and some ordinary people, would want to maintain that some ideal values have an independent existence: in other words, that there are some things which are ultimately worth valuing or ultimately valuable independently of whether or not anyone values them. Other philosophers, while not necessarily wanting to endorse the view that there *are* self-subsistent values, maintain that we incorrigibly *speak* as though there are – that part of what distinguishes a man's ideal values from his liking values is his regarding them as things which are valuable or properly to be valued quite independently of him. Fortunately, we need not for our present purposes debate these questions, which are concerned with the objectivity of value and the proper analysis of value judgment. It is sufficient for our purposes to note that people do in fact have ideal values as well as liking values.

Of course, if someone refuses to speak in terms of objective values he cannot reasonably say that the ideal values which others have are wrong, or right for that matter; such judgments presuppose a belief in objective values. What he can do, if other people's ideal values run counter to his own, is to point out where their ideal values involve them in inconsistencies or in policies which they may find unacceptable. And in so far as we embark on any criticism of the value bases of medicine and social work it will be of this kind.

It may now be maintained that there are some ideal values which everyone must share because the facts of human life embody them. For example, it may be said that the facts of human physical vulnerability entail the ideal value of compassion. But this is not so. It is true that if human beings were not vulnerable there could be no such thing as compassion. But there is a logical gap between the judgment that men suffer and the judgment that we ought to pity and help them. Indeed, a Nietzschean philosophy would maintain that we ought *not* to help them, that what is important is strength and ability and it is slavish to set great store by the weak; and actual military societies, such as Sparta, seem not to have set store by compassion.

Even if we all shared the same basic ideal values, however, there would still be disagreements about how to apply them and what to do when they conflict. For example, two doctors who agree on holding the sanctity of life as an ideal value may still disagree on whether to remove life-support systems from a patient in an irreversible coma. The facts – that he will not recover, that his brain is irretrievably damaged, that the equipment is needed elsewhere – may all be agreed, but one cannot feed these into a moral computer and get out an answer about what ought to be done. Again, two social workers may agree on the ideal values of autonomy and self-development. But in a case where these two conflict, for example, where a youth in care or on probation wants to abandon an apprenticeship and go into a well-paid dead-end job, the social workers may differ about whether he should be allowed to make his own decisions or pressurized into remaining in the position of greater opportunity for extending himself.

The upshot of these remarks is that the value base of medicine and social work is in a sense ultimately independent of the knowledge base. Whatever is discovered about human beings, their minds and bodies, the effect on them of organisms and substances within and pressures without, questions of value will still remain matters for discussion which cannot be *proven* one way or the other, though widespread agreement may be reached.

The aims of the caring professions as embodying values

We shall now attempt to show how values, of both the liking and ideal kinds, are involved in the aims of the caring professions. We are referring to what may be called the *intrinsic* aims of these professions: that is, the aims which a doctor has *as* doctor or a social worker has *as* social worker.[2] These must be distinguished, both from the *personal* aims that a particular worker may have which are not necessarily shared by others in the profession and which he might have pursued in another profession; and from the *extrinsic* aims which a particular worker may pursue as a *result* of being a member of his profession but which go beyond it. For example, a particular social worker may have as his personal aims earning a living and sublimating deviant sexual tendencies, and as his extrinsic aim the 'cleaning-up' of a corrupt local authority.

The intrinsic aims, by contrast, might seem to be those which all social workers pursue as part of their job. But this is not quite accurate. A disillusioned and embittered social worker might simply aim to do the least that would keep him in his job, and clearly we cannot judge the intrinsic aims of social work by such a man. The intrinsic aims of social work are the aims of those who are trying to be good social workers and to meet the needs which social workers are employed to serve. These aims provide the answer to the questions 'What is the point of social work?' and 'Why do we need social workers?' and therefore they also consti- tute the aims people have in employing social workers. The same will apply to medicine too, except that in some cases of medicine, viz., private medicine, the employers and the needers of service are the same people, whereas in social work they will almost never be, since the clients of social work are typically without resources and so unable to employ anyone themselves.

It might now be objected that in medicine, at any rate, there is *no* one intrinsic aim: the aims of a private patient and of a Lord Beveridge are quite different in *kind*, since the private patient is interested only in his own health whereas Beveridge has a philan- thropic concern for the general good. But of course Beveridge was interested in health as well. The setting-up of a health service involves a combination of *two* ideas: a philanthropic idea, about service to all or to the general good, plus an idea about the importance of health for that good. These are separate notions: it is quite possible to have philanthropic ideas, but to see the good of man only in terms of his spiritual salvation. Conversely, it is quite possible to pursue health without any conception of an obligation to extend the benefit to all, however disadvantaged.

We have been speaking just now of the intrinsic *aims* rather than intrinsic *values* of medicine and social work. But in the case of the philanthropic ideal which forms one component of the aims of health and welfare services, we clearly have an aim which is for many an ideal value as well, for the idea is that those in need *ought* to be helped, not just because the helpers want to do so, but because the needy make a claim on us. This idea has taken various forms. For instance, it has been seen as a Christian duty enjoined by the founder of the faith, as an expression of Christian love of our neighbour ('charity') or more recently as the recognition of a so-called *human right* to basic welfare, this last conception rejecting the notion of an optional extra, or act of supererogation going beyond strict duty, which sometimes gets attached to charity.[3]

As we have seen, this value of philanthropy is more inextricably bound up with social work than with medicine. If social work is to exist at all, there have to be either private philanthropists or a state system of imposing philanthropy on the general public by means of taxes, since the beneficiaries are not in a position to finance the service. For medicine, on the other hand, there need only be people who need the services of a doctor for themselves and have the money to pay him. Note, however, that this difference lies in the method of supporting the two professions, rather than in the motivation of their practitioners, and provides no reason why a social worker should be any more or less altruistic than a doctor.

We said that there were *two* ideas present in the notion of a health service: philanthropy, and the idea of health as part of man's good. Similarly the social services incorporate the philanthropic idea plus an idea of human *welfare*. We have then the two notions of health and welfare to describe those aspects of human good which the philanthropic institutions, the health and social services, aim to foster. In what sense are health and welfare *values*? This is in fact quite a complex question. First of all they are liking values for all those who want them and value them for their own sakes. We shall see in the next section why someone might want health for its own sake, as distinct from its usefulness. Welfare, like 'good' itself, is a much vaguer word; but in one sense, that of 'interests', it must by definition be a liking value of everyone, since 'interests' is simply a blanket-term for all someone's liking values, and on this meaning welfare would normally include health as one of its components. The connection between these liking values and the ideal value of philanthropy is that philanthropic people are those who have the ideal of helping others to attain their liking values – and the means to them, health being just as important under this head too. This aspect of philanthropy construes human good in terms of what people want.

But sometimes 'health' and 'welfare' stand for ideal values which the doctor and social worker possess and try to pass on to the client or patient. Whereas the doctor or social worker who was interested only in clients' *wants* will regard himself as having no task to perform if the client is happy, those who have ideal values of health and welfare will feel that it is part of the social worker's or doctor's role to promote the pursuit of these things for their own sakes, whether or not their clients want them now. Thus, for example, a social worker might see his client's power to make his own decisions as part of his welfare, to be sought not only if the client wanted it but also if he was content to lean on others. Such doctors or social workers are still thinking of their clients' *good*, but seeing it in terms of what we may call their *improvement* – an ideal conception of how people ought to be which may or may not be shared as an ideal by the client.

The foregoing example brings out again the 'blank cheque' nature of the idea of welfare. Just as welfare as a liking value meant 'whatever someone happens to want for its own sake', so 'welfare' as an ideal value means 'whatever state is thought to be good for its possessor'. Health, by contrast, is a notion with more definite content, at least so far as *physical* health goes: *mental* health, as we shall see, can similarly be given a precise content, but can also be a blank cheque for whatever good aspects of personality and character the speaker has among his ideal values.

Before we go on to consider health and welfare in more detail, however, we must try to meet two fundamental objections to our conclusions so far. The first objection is a kind of accusation of *pretentiousness*. We have assumed that health and welfare are *values*. But it might be objected that the end-products of a great many occupations are just as important as health or welfare, without anyone feeling the need to attach such grandiose names as 'values' to them. For example, the farmer's end-product is food, which is of fundamental importance to human welfare, but no one speaks of the value base of farming.

A cynical reply would be that this is because farmers are less pretentious people than doctors and social workers, and also feel less need (than social workers, at least) to justify their activity. But a more satisfactory answer is also possible. Food is not valuable in *itself*; it is valuable because it is necessary for sustaining life. But health can be, and welfare necessarily is, seen as valuable in *itself*. Moreover, both have an aspect of the ideal about them, which food does not have. The production of food, then, cannot be taken as a value in this sense. Of course the farmer may have the *extrinsic* aim of serving the nation's health, and in this he is subscribing to the values of health and of philanthropy. He may also have *personal* aims which represent values of his: respect for the beauty of the countryside, for example. But the intrinsic aim of the farmer is a means, not an end. This does not mean that the farmer is less important than the doctor; it is true that the farmer deals in food, not in health as such, but there cannot be health without food whereas there can be health without medicine. The same kind of reply, *mutatis mutandis*, can be made to anyone who says that a plumber's work is as conducive to human welfare as a social worker's without having all this fuss about *values* made about it.

The other objection attacks the idea that social services are *philanthropic* systems, designed for the good of their beneficiaries. On the contrary, it is argued, they are systems of social control aimed at preventing revolution by providing palliatives for the worst miseries and so distracting the attention of the unfortunate from the basic injustice of the present system which has caused their plight.

The first point to make in reply to this objection is to distinguish motive and result. It may be the case that welfare services do make people more contented with an unjust position in society than they would otherwise be, but it does not follow that this is the *motive* of those who set up the systems or of those who work them. And it is rather implausible to believe this is a likely motivation, not only because appearances are so thoroughly against the view, but also because tough-minded wordly wisdom would if anything recommend the opposite policy: 'Give 'em an inch and they take an ell'. As for result, it might well be that the beneficiaries of a Welfare State will not feel the desperation which drives revolutionaries to drastic measures. But if the services have been successful they should be healthy, independent, educated, balanced people who have a sharp sense of their rights and a knowledge of ways to go about securing them; for, as we shall see, the social worker aims to make his client mature, autonomous and self-respecting.

It may be objected that these rights are still those of an iniquitous system, and that the doctor and social worker, instead of propping up this system by endorsing it, should if they are truly philanthropic be encouraging their clients to destroy it. Of course social workers do sometimes encourage clients in illegal practices such as squatting. But urging their clients to revolution would go against the idea of helping *individuals*, for if there were any benefits to society resulting from a revolution, they would not solve the problems of these people here and now. To advocate revolution as the cure for specific ills is to put 'society' before the individual whose welfare is the essence of social work and whose plight calls for compassion. Of course the worker may have as an *extrinsic* aim the promotion of a more just society. He may even, consistently with his profession as social worker, be plotting to achieve this by a revolution. But *qua* social worker, his duty is to his clients as individuals and his task to find the most practical way of helping them here and now.

The concept of health

Health, as popularly conceived, is part of not one but two oppositions: that between health and disease or illness, on the one hand, and that between good and poor health, on the other. Disease and illness are, broadly speaking, seen as *episodes* interrupting health, which is restored when the illness is past, whereas poor health is a long-lasting, perhaps life-long, state involving a disposition to become ill easily. A healthy person is one who does not suffer from poor health in this sense, and thus a person can be described as *healthy* at a time when he is ill, if what is meant is that he is not often ill. This distinction is obviously not sharp. For example, someone can be described as in poor health if he has some chronic disease which means both that he is not quite well and also that he is especially prone to get other diseases. But there are some clear cases where poor health is due not to disease but to some other factor, e.g. a poor organ such as a defective heart, or malnutrition. The medical profession is obviously concerned with health in both these senses.

We have defined both kinds of health negatively, in terms of the absence of disease or illness, so the next stage is to give an account of disease or illness. The first thing to note is that the two terms are not synonymous. A person can be said to be ill without having a disease: if he is clinically depressed, if he has taken an overdose, if he is suffering from shock, or if (at least according to

BBC news bulletin vocabulary) he has been shot or blown up and is 'in a critical condition'. Again, someone can have a disease without being ill, as in the case of minor skin diseases. Now to describe the doctor's work in terms either of disease or of illness would be incomplete without mention of the other; clearly a doctor is professionally interested both in those suffering from overdoses or shock and in those suffering from minor skin ailments. We shall therefore have to give an account of health in terms of both notions. Let us explore their meaning and relationship further.

Illness is a less technical notion than disease: any lay person, including the sufferer himself, can know that someone is ill without knowing whether or not he has a disease, let alone what disease he has. At least, this is true of physical illness; mental illness may be more difficult. Taking physical illness only for the time being, let us consider what makes someone say he or another person is ill. The kind of things which are relevant are what may be called *overall upsets of the system*: for example, not wanting to eat or not being able to digest; feeling and being weak; feeling abnormally hot or cold; in serious cases, being unconscious or semi-conscious, with weak pulse. (It is the last kind of condition which is presumably referred to when victims of attacks are said to be ill.) People who are ill will often have headaches or rashes or itches but these would not constitute being ill without the central phenomena; thus someone can say 'When I had German measles I came out in a splendid rash but I wasn't *ill* at all' – meaning that he was not (or not very) feverish, ate normally, felt strong, etc. Again, someone who has a stye or boil is not ill simply thereby, although if he gets a fever as a result of this kind of infection, he is then said to be ill.

So far we have made no distinction between *being* ill and *feeling* ill. But the sense of the distinction is far from clear. One distinction might be between those things of which only the sufferer is aware – aches and pains, feelings of faintness or nausea – and things which can be detected by others, such as raised temperature or quickened pulse. If a patient reports a series of untoward feelings but the doctor can 'find nothing', he might say, 'You aren't really ill'. Similarly, the person with German measles who has a rash but feels fine, instead of saying 'I'm not ill' as in our earlier example, might equally say 'I don't *feel* ill', implying that since he has German measles he *is* in fact ill. But this distinction between the objective and the subjective conditions is not an exhaustive account of the difference between being ill and feeling ill. For if someone *goes on* reporting headaches, giddiness and so on of sufficient severity, and we believe him, we might well say, not just that he feels ill, but that he *is* ill with some as yet mysterious condition. Of course, many a doctor in such a case will say (or at any rate think), 'You're not really ill, it's just your nerves.' But then the same view could be expressed, perhaps more charitably, by saying, 'It's your nerves which are making you ill.' The distinction, then, is sometimes between the objective and the subjective, sometimes between the temporary and the persistent, sometimes between the physical and the mental.

Disease is a more technical notion than illness, as we said earlier. A person who has a *disease* suffers from some condition which is identifiable as similar to that suffered by some others and with the same cause. The cause may not be *known*, but the assumption is made that there is a specific virus, or fungus, or a deficiency of diet or gland, or whatever it may be, which is causing the disorder. With disease, as opposed to illness, the disorder may be minor and localized, as with a trivial skin disease such as impetigo.

The crucial notion in our account of both illness and disease, that which sets both in opposition to health, is that of *upset* and *disorder*. We can partly understand this if we think of the human body as a machine, in which various *processes* (such as digestion and excretion, maintenance of a certain temperature, inhalation of oxygen) necessary to its maintenance and smooth working are carried out, and through which the person whose body it is carries out his actions. On this model an upset or disorder would be some failure in the system which prevented the machine from working properly, and what was wrong or bad about it would be precisely this interference with the machine's normal working.

But this model is only partly satisfactory. For one thing, it does not accommodate *pain* and other subjective symptoms, such as nausea, feeling faint, etc. It might be retorted that this is in the nature of the case, since pain and the other feelings are essentially inward and non-mechanistic. In any case, it might be said, they are *signs* of the disorder rather than parts of it, and so their analogue in mechanical terms would be with the untoward sounds with which motorists become obsessed. But this will not quite do either. There can be pains with no apparent organic cause, and in a case like this we would *not* say 'Since the mechanism is working normally that's all that matters.' The pain itself constitutes a disorder which must be put right. No doubt if severe it will interfere psychologically with the sufferer's activities, but even where it does not, the presence of pain is still in itself a matter for medical attention, and a person in pain, even with no apparent cause, is regarded as ill or at any rate not well.

So far, then, we have two kinds of phenomenon which constitute the kind of disorder which makes us say a person is not in good health: what may be termed 'mechanical failure', and pain or other discomfort. Is there any way of linking these two factors? One possible link which suggests itself, since illness and disease are *bad* things, is that both pain and malfunction are *unpleasant* things for those who have them. This assertion, of course, needs a little qualification. Some pain, in some circumstances, can be pleasant, and illness can be positively welcome – if, for example, it gets one out of the army. But in general terms pain is unpleasant, and in general being incapacitated prevents a person from doing whatever he wants to do, assuming he is a normal person with normal plans and projects.

Can we then say that the disorder which characterizes illness and disease, and which takes the forms both of discomfort and of mechanical failure, is to be defined as a (physical) condition which is in general unpleasant or prevents a man from doing what he wants? This will not do, for there are examples of such conditions which are clearly not illnesses: for instance, the weakness and loss of faculties which accompany ageing. These are not regarded as illnesses because they are 'natural' or 'normal': in other words, everyone goes through something of the kind, or at any rate suffers some out of a range of unpleasant changes. There is therefore an idea of the *normal* against which certain kinds of change are judged to be illnesses, others not. In a similar way, the pains of childbirth, arising as they do from a natural process, are regarded as normal.

We can say, then, that a condition is to be regarded as a disorder, and not merely unpleasant, by reference to a conception of a normal state for human beings. The aspect of abnormality is indeed uppermost in some cases of disease. As we said earlier, minor skin diseases may not make a person ill in any way or cause any discomfort, and what makes them *diseases* is that they constitute abnormal conditions of the skin. Of course they are as a rule *undesirable* to their possessor, because they are ugly, but the verdict of ugliness is largely dependent on the judgment of abnormality.

At this point it may well be objected that to distinguish normal from abnormal changes and call only the latter illnesses and diseases is totally artificial, as doctors are also concerned with trying to arrest 'normal' changes if they are undesirable: for example, using hormone therapy to lessen the effects of ageing. But this is not just a question of definition. If a young child has stiff joints we would say there is something *wrong* with him, whereas if an old person has stiff joints we would say instead that he is not as agile as he was. But there is a difference not only in how the two situations are described, but also in how they are dealt with. No doubt doctors do try to alleviate such concomitants of old age, but there would be much more doubt about spending a lot of effort on such activity than there would be in the case of the child, if the two disabilities are equal, because there is an idea that older people 'shouldn't expect' to be as mobile as they were. A parallel situation occurs with regard to deformity and ugliness. Certainly doctors do regard it as part of their business to correct ugliness (with plastic surgery) if the ugliness is extreme, but if it is mild it does not seem to make the automatic claim for aid that a deformity such as a hare-lip does. Similarly, they will regard it as their business to relieve the pains of childbirth where these are extreme, but not to remove all trace of discomfort.

In our conception of disease and illness, then, there is a built-in reference to some normal condition of the human body by reference to which these things are aberrations; and doctors regard themselves as especially concerned with putting right these abnormalities. No doubt the answer to the question 'Why put them right?' would usually be in terms of the unpleasantness of the condition rather than its abnormality. Thus a disease which had no signs or symptoms other than turning hair blonde might be one of which people did not seek to be cured. But it would still be a disease in a way that natural greying is not.

We have said that deformity is analogous to illness in being a disorder which medicine is concerned to treat – or better still, of course, to prevent. But it should be noticed that deformity, unlike illness and disease, is not *as such* incompatible with good health. Of course there are some deformities, such as 'a hole in the heart', which produce mechanical failures like those of illness, and a sufferer from these is said to be in poor health, as we saw earlier. But a 'thalidomide baby' who has only vestigial limbs can still be described as *healthy*. Similarly, a child who is born with a malformation of the ears which makes him deaf is not called unhealthy. It is true that a person who is severely handicapped in this way might hesitate before stating on a form that he is in good health, but broadly speaking these handicaps, severe though they are, are somehow not thought of as impairing health. This is difficult to understand in terms of our account so far, which depicts health as freedom from uncomfortable or frustrating abnormalities.

The explanation seems to be that illness and disease are seen as things which essentially progress or change in a law-like manner (cf. chapter 4), which have a life of their own. (Of course, they usually have literally a life of their own, in the sense of being caused by invading organisms, but a person can be ill without any such cause, as in cases of psychosomatic illness.) In such cases one can always sensibly ask whether the sufferer is getting better or worse. Being ill is essentially an *unstable* situation. The thalidomide victim, by contrast, is fixed in his disability, and so he is not regarded as unhealthy because there is nothing untoward *going on* in him. But the fact, if it is one, that the deformed person is not regarded as *unhealthy* does not mean that doctors have no concern with trying to prevent such cases or to alleviate their lot with false limbs, plastic surgery, etc. What it shows, rather, is that health, as that concept is normally employed, is too *narrow* to be regarded as the goal of medicine. What we need instead is some notion of physical 'wholeness' which includes not only what is covered by the notion of health but also freedom from deformity.

Some of the points which apply to deformity apply also to *injury*. Sometimes a person who has been badly injured is described as *ill*, and when this is so he is suffering from the same kinds of incapacity that attend other illness – he is weak, faint, unconscious, etc. But if the lack of capacity is simply the essential result of the injury, then the sufferer is not ill, and might in one sense be in good health: a skier who has broken his leg cannot walk, but he may be in glowing health. The doctor's task here may again be described as the restoration not of health but of wholeness. But injury is in one respect more like illness than like deformity: it admits of *progress* in that it can *heal*. In fact the old-fashioned or religious-sounding noun 'healing' covers more of the ground required for the aim of medicine than our common modern word 'health'.

So far, then, we have depicted the aim of medicine as the promotion not just of health as the word is normally used, but of 'wholeness'. This we have defined *negatively*, as freedom from abnormal and unwanted conditions, whether these are static, as with deformities, or progressive as with illnesses and injuries. But there can also be a positive aspect to health: not merely absence of discomfort and incapacity, but the positive feelings of a sense of fitness and energy, and a supple and well-tuned body (again mechanical terms seem appropriate) – the condition in which someone is said to glow with health, be bursting with health and so on. What may be seen as a luxury from the point of view of the negative aspect of health, such as the promotion of vigour in old age, is central from the point of view of the positive aspect. Medical concern with *contraception* can perhaps also be classified as the promotion of positive health; in general neither pregnancy nor abstinence constitute or produce *ill*-health, but any doctor who says his patient must choose between them is ignoring one element of physical pleasure and well-being. (He would normally of course say this, if at all, in the name of another *ideal*, and might even say that nothing which is against God's law, say, can count as physical well-being. But it would be less mis-leading for him to say that physical well-being is not the most important kind of well-being.)

Mental health

Our account of health in the previous section said nothing about *mental* health. This is a notoriously difficult idea to define, for reasons which will become apparent when we try to apply the ideas we have gleaned so far of health as the absence of abnormal and unwanted conditions. Consider first abnormality. The norm of states of mind is a much less obvious thing than the norm of bodily states. Whereas there is general agreement as to when someone is *physically* ill, there can be widespread disagreement as to what is a normal state of *mind*. Indeed, the suggestion that anyone who has an abnormal state of mind is mentally ill could be taken to construe as forms of mental illness both immorality and non-conformity with the prevailing social and political regime. Moreover, some psychiatrists are happy to accept this idea. Consider for example the following: 'It should be stressed that all failure to comply with the rules of the game, and indeed all anti-social behaviour, ... is evidence of some psychological failure in the conduct of life.'[4] By thus construing any 'deviant' behaviour as the product of illness, such psychiatrists give a spurious air of objectivity to what is largely culture-relative and deny responsibility for action to those they regard as wrongdoers. The extreme of such a view is seen in those Russian psychiatrists who treat as mentally ill those who criticize the Soviet regime – or at least this is their view if they are sincere.

The idea of mental illness as an *unwanted* state is just as difficult. In the case of physical illness it is the sufferer himself who does not want the condition in which he finds himself. But in the case of mental illness, it might be argued, what is wrong may precisely be that the sufferer is content with the state he is in: in other words, he may have diseased wants. The psychopath, for example, is not unhappy about the frightful things he does and what is wrong with him is just this; it is other people who actually suffer from his state, not the 'sufferer' himself.

Antony Flew, in his book *Crime or Disease?*, rejects these ideas, that the mentally-ill man is a 'deviant' and that a man may be said to have diseased wants.[5] His reasons for doing so are not only that this line of thinking construes anyone sufficiently unconventional as mentally ill, but also that it does not explain how mental illness can be an *excuse* (since excuses appeal to compulsion or ignorance); that it does not square with what he calls the conceptual point that mental illness, if it is to be called *illness*, must by definition be unwelcome to the sufferer himself; and that it gives a dangerous licence for compulsory 'cure', since the doctors can always argue that it must by definition be in a person's interest to be cured of a disease.

To make these points, Flew sets up a narrow definition of mental illness in terms of loss of *capacity*.[6] Just as (he says) physical disease means that the body or parts of it cannot fulfil its function, so mental disease means that a man cannot do what he is normally able to do in the mental sphere, viz., reason, understand his world, exercise his will. On this account, paradigms of mental illness are obsessive neuroses (manifesting themselves in actions which the patient *cannot help* doing) or other compulsive conditions; psychopathology, on the other hand, manifesting itself in frightful *behaviour* which the agent deliberately and willingly carries out, is not a mental illness at all – a conclusion which Flew welcomes, since he sees no reason to excuse the psychopath.

The first point to notice here is that even in the case of straightforward physical illness, doctors are not at liberty to cure someone against his will just because it must be in his interests to be cured; so even if psychiatrists could make out that all sorts of untoward states of mind are illnesses and somehow by definition against their possessor's interests, this would in no way license compulsory cure. We need not therefore feel that the scope of mental illness must be narrowed to those conditions for which the sufferer himself would seek relief.

The second point to notice is that we can allow that *some* mental illness absolves people from responsibility, but not all: for example, we can say that the compulsive arsonist is not responsible for what he does because he is sick and cannot help it, whereas the psychopath *is* responsible because he *can* help it and what is sick about him is his having the desires he has. Of course it may be that the psychopath is after all *not* responsible, if for example his desires are uncontrollably strong, or if he is incapable of understanding the true nature of what he does. But there is nothing incoherent in the idea that a person may have sick wishes (not merely bad ones) and choose to act on them and be responsible for that choice. Flew seems to start from the premise: 'All mental illness excuses'; from which it follows, either that the psychopath is excused, which Flew does not want, or that he is not mentally ill. But if we reject the premise we can allow, as seems intuitively plausible, that there are such things as desires which are in themselves sick: for example, the desire to torture children.

There are, however, the two difficulties noted earlier with the idea that some desires are in themselves sick: the difficulty of 'drawing the line' without making mental health just a matter of conformity, and the difficulty of showing how a mental illness which consists of deviant desires is something which a man necessarily has reason not to want. Both these problems do not arise with Flew's 'paradigm cases' of mental illness, the cases of loss of mental capacity.

On the question of drawing the line, we can say only that a sick desire is something that people in general cannot reasonably make any sense of in terms of their own desires. This may seem hopelessly conservative, but note, first, that we are not saying that anyone with a sick desire, as such, is a fit subject for *interference*: what is punishable is not desire but action. Note, second, that we are not saying that people in general must *have* the desire in question in order to make sense of it. Thus people in general do not have a desire to have sex with those of their own sex, but they can reasonably (i.e. if they think about it and use their imaginations) make sense of the desire to do so if they think of the links between sex and affection or friendship or admiration of beauty in their own experience, and of any intense feelings they have felt for others of their own sex. On the other hand, the desire to collect little pieces of fluff will seem to bear no relation to any of the reasons for which people collect things. It is of course true, as Flew says, that everyone knows what it is to want something. But this does not make it comprehensible to want just anything, any more than the experience of believing things enables us to understand how a person can believe that he is made of glass.

Note, third, that there is on this account, as there must be, a difference between a sick desire and an immoral one. We can perfectly well hold that it is *sick* to want to have sex with one's dog but not *immoral* (if the dog would like it), whereas it is immoral, but not sick, to want to have sex with a colleague's spouse. Note, fourth, that on this kind of criterion the sickness of desires is bound to be a matter of degree. Some desires will apparently bear no connection with anything that anyone else desires. Others will make some sort of sense to most people but the connection with sense will be rather far-fetched.

The second difficulty with allowing that some 'deviant' desires are indications of mental sickness was that a sickness is supposed to be something which by definition the sick man does not want. Now even with physical disease this connection may be weak; as we saw in the case of minor skin diseases, it may be that the main reason for not wanting them is simply that they are diseases, rather than that the main reason for their being diseases is that people do not want them. In a similar way, someone who is haunted by fantasies of making love to a dog may wish to be rid of them simply because he thinks of them as sick: abnormal, in the sense we have described. Where a person has desires which other people regard as sick but which he himself is quite happy about, we can say that he would have reason to dislike them, as sick, if he understood their nature. This line of thought carries with it in itself no licence to interfere with anyone's sick desires, as we have said already.

We have then a twofold account of mental illness, in terms of loss of mental capacity and/or possession of deviant desires. On this account, many people see psychiatrists regularly, especially in the USA, without being mentally ill at all; rather, for example, they wish to discuss the problems they are experiencing in their marriages. We could see this practice either as the counterpart of the physical doctor's promotion of positive health, or more plausibly as a use of the doctor's expertise in spheres which are not strictly concerned with *health* at all, but in which nevertheless he has a special competence; rather as in the bodily sphere an athlete who is agreed to be in excellent health might consult a doctor about his inability to manage some particular series of movements, on the grounds that the doctor is incidentally an expert on anatomy. In other words, if a psychiatrist is to be seen as a *doctor*, helping sick people, he is stepping outside his role if he counsels miserable people instead – which is not to say that such counselling is not worth doing.

Health as a value

The answer to the questions why and in what senses health, physical and mental, is a *value* is quite complex. One reason why health is valuable is of course obvious: freedom from incapacitating physical or mental illness is valuable because it is *useful*; it enables the person who has that freedom to carry out his purposes, whatever these may be, and the same is true of freedom from incapacitating injury or deformity. There is no one who does not have reason to want health for the usefulness of it, whatever his projects in life. Admittedly, there may be circumstances where someone is glad of ill-health as the lesser of two evils, as when it saves him from military service of a dangerous kind. But ill-health even in these circumstances is regrettable, given the possibilities that it cuts off.

What we have said so far makes health valuable only as a means, not as an end, and so not a value in the sense defined at the beginning of the chapter. (This does not make it not really valuable; on the contrary, most things which are values, in that they are valued for their own sakes, depend on health for their full enjoyment.) The second reason for valuing health, however, makes health valued not for what it brings but for what it is: health is desirable because sickness is *painful*. This is the reason for health's being a good which Hume gives in his *Enquiry*, and he regards it as a reason which puts an end to further questioning.[7] We can amplify this point by recalling the positive *pleasures* – glows of fitness and so on – which attend the peak of health.

The *scope* of this second reason is of course limited, since not all forms of absence of health are painful, even in a wider sense of 'painful' which includes 'uncomfortable' and 'distressing'. There is also what might be called a limitation in *depth*, in that if health is valued for this reason, viz., pleasure and absence of pain, it is not being regarded as something to be *approved* of, but simply as something to be wanted for its own sake. In terms of the distinction we drew at the beginning of the chapter, it is a liking value rather than an ideal value.

It is also possible, we submit, to value health in a third way, to regard it as an ideal to be sought after, in such a way that people who cherish health are to be approved of and people who squander it are to be disapproved of. Aristotle distinguished three types of thing which people desire: the useful, the pleasant and the noble. Health can be desired under all three heads. It is easy to explain, as we have done, how it can be desired under the first two. To explain the third is more difficult. But it is perhaps a biological and teleological or purposive idea of how our species is '*meant*' to be which catches people's imaginations. It is partly an aesthetic idea, of a *design* with which we ought to conform, and in terms of which aberrations are seen as ugly: we suggested earlier that people can dislike conditions in themselves, and see them as ugly, simply because they see them as unhealthy.

There are various ways of explaining this idea of health as an ideal. It might rest on belief in a wise and good God whose creative blueprint we can try to exemplify as perfectly as possible, and from whom we hold our bodies and minds in trust and to whom we have a duty to keep them in good repair. It is worth noting, however, that a religious approach to health does not necessarily produce this conclusion. There are some strands in religious thinking in terms of which the body is depicted as evil, and the flesh as something to be mortified rather than preserved. From this point of view a believer might thank God for his ill-health as something which keeps him from evil.

A secular approach might be in terms of respect for the species: it might be said that it is incumbent on us as human beings to make our human nature flourish. This is an idea which goes back to Plato, and it has perennial appeal. J.S. Mill states it as follows:

> Human nature is not a machine to be built after a model, and set to do exactly the work prescribed for it, but a tree, which requires to grow and develop on all sides according to the tendency of the inward forces which make it a living thing.[8]

It is true that Plato and Mill were apt to see human nature in mainly intellectual terms. But one might with equal plausibility see a person as a mind/body unity; and even if it *is* in virtue of his intellect that Man is thought of as a superior species, this assessment once arrived at might seem to entail some reverence for the species of body which contains this intellect. At all events we suggest that the value people place upon health *as such*, apart from both its usefulness and its pleasantness, is a kind of ideal value, representing the source of strong feeling in some people. Plato was appealing to some such feeling when he said that justice could be shown to be valuable in itself, not only for its results, if it was seen as a *healthy* state of soul.[9] Though we would reject this notion of justice, which implies that the unjust man is sick, we can agree with one implication of Plato's argument, that health can be seen as in itself desirable.

To many people, however, including many health workers, these considerations will seem hopelessly 'high-falutin''. For them, health is important simply because it is useful and its absence is painful. Their conception of others' good, at any rate in so far as they are to be instrumental in promoting it, is in terms of enabling those others to get whatever *they* want, not of some ideal which patients are to be encouraged to pursue. Such health workers see their task as like that of the farmer whose role we discussed earlier. And, as we said earlier, the farmer is no less important because the purpose he serves is to provide something useful rather than good in itself.

The concept of welfare

As we saw earlier, 'welfare' is a word with two possible interpretations: it can mean either 'interests' or 'improvement in character, personality, etc.' In this ambiguity it is like 'good', when used in phrases like 'thinking of the good of others', and indeed there can be a tendency to push even the word 'interests' from its proper side to the other – a tendency which we hope we can resist, as it makes for confusion.

In their proper sense, then, interests are to do with the *desires* of the person whose interests they are said to be: something is in a person's interests if it will bring him what he wants, or of course remove what he wants to get rid of. Notice that we say '*bring* him what he wants', rather than '*is* what he wants'. This is because the notion of interests implies a kind of calculation of the whole range of a person's wants. Thus if it is in a boy's interests to have a motorcycle, this means, not just that he wants the motorcycle, but that it will enable him to get or do a range of things – save money on fares, go to sports events at a distance, etc. If he wants the motorcycle but it is *not* in his interests to have it, this means that (for example) he could spend the money more profitably on something else, or is too likely to get injured.

This sketch of interests might suggest that a thing cannot be said to be part of a person's interests on the ground that it is itself wanted for its own sake. But this would be a mistake. If something in this category is so important that clearly *any* set of things wanted must give it a prominent place, then it can be said to be in someone's interests. Thus we can say that it is obviously in a child's interests not to get battered, and this is basically because pain is something which everyone wants to avoid for its own sake.

It is not so obvious that it is in his interests to be taken away from his battering parents. This would depend on a *calculation* of what he would gain and what he would lose by being taken away.

This example may prompt a question about the difference between interests and *needs*, since we could also say that a child *needs* protection from physical assault. The relation seems to be that needs are a specially important range of interests, those without which we judge that a reasonable human life cannot be lived. Thus we might say of a particular child that he *needs* to be taken away from his family who neglect him and that it would be in his *interests* to be fostered rather than go to a children's home (if we say he *needs* to be fostered, this is a stronger statement, and suggests either a severe criticism of this or all children's homes or a lack of emotional and personal development in the child which it is thought that a children's home cannot help).

It might be objected that this difference between needs and other interests is in practice non-existent: *anything* can be spoken of as a need, however frivolous, as when a teenager says 'I need some black lipstick for the newest Grot Look'. This objection can however be met by drawing a distinction between absolute and relative needs. It is true that anything can be said to be needed *relative* to a particular purpose: black lipstick is needed for looking like a Grot, or whatever. But nobody needs black lipstick absolutely, that is to say, for a reasonable human life, whatever the teenager may maintain; and it is this latter notion of needs which we have been comparing with interests. Of course, these so-called absolute needs are to some extent relative in another sense: relative to society's opinion of what constitutes a reasonable human life. The boundary between a need and an interest which is not a need is shifting all the time; holidays with pay, once unheard of, are now described as a human right, which suggests they are now thought of as a need.

Our account of the relationship between interests and needs might however be attacked from another point of view. We said needs were a very important kind of interest, and then defined 'needs' in terms of the conception of a reasonable human life. But it might well be said that this latter conception has moved away from the actual wants in terms of which we defined interests towards some ideal of what human beings, whatever they want, *ought* to be like. For example, we might say that no reasonable human life is possible without relationships with other human beings, and then in the light of this dictum pronounce that some old person who lives as a recluse *needs* companionship, even if he says he does not want the company of others.

The answer to this objection lies in a careful drawing of distinctions. The notion of a reasonable life can be seen in terms of what makes people *happy*. A person can be contented, in an apathetic depressed kind of way, with a way of life which is far from making him happy; and if what is lacking in such a person's life is something sufficiently fundamental and general in its appeal, it will be quite plausible for others to say (still within the basic framework of wants) that he needs it in the sense that he would be immeasurably happier with it, even if he himself does not realize this. It will also be true to say that his life will be enormously *improved* according to most people's ideas of the good life, but this is a separate claim. The language of needs and interests is sometimes used to make this claim too, but as we have seen it makes for clarity to resist this usage in the present discussion.

We have, then, a picture of a person's interests as consisting of whatever meets his own wishes, taken as a whole and with regard to the future as well as the present, his needs being those parts of his interests which are most central and important. Clearly, on this definition of 'needs' there will be some variation in individuals' needs, but also a good deal of similarity if we believe in constant features of human nature.

Is the promotion of interests, thus conceived, the one aim of the social worker? Clearly many of his activities *can* be seen as promoting the interests of his clients (or more particularly their *needs*, since resources are limited and he cannot hope to foster the whole scope of their interests). For example, he will settle needy families in housing, make sure they get the welfare benefits due to them, look for sources of supply of needed goods such as prams or stoves, rescue battered children from their parents or wives from their husbands, find homes or Homes for abandoned children and children for those with a home to give them. All these activities fall squarely within the scope of *interests* as we have defined them, being concerned with things people want.

But there are other things at which social workers typically aim which contain elements of the 'improvement' sense of welfare.

For example, they seek to improve their clients' capacity for meaningful family and personal relationships by fostering their self-knowledge and their understanding of others. Now this may be seen simply as likely to make the client *happier*. But it is also described as an independent ideal in terms of the cultivation of a mature personality and so on. And in general the social worker aims to make his clients autonomous or independent, able to plan their own lives and take their own decisions without recourse to him. Again, it *might* be true that this autonomy is looked on as in the clients' interests. But it would often be more in their *interests* to have a (presumably) intelligent, capable and knowledgeable person running things for them, especially if they like him and want things to stay as they are. In such a case, autonomy is in the clients' interests only in the other, non-wants, sense of interests, viz., in the sense in which development of autonomy is seen as an *improvement* in the clients' personality. A social worker may try to persuade a client to get a job instead of staying on the dole, in cases where in terms of sheer financial reward the balance of interest is pretty evenly poised, because he feels that working is somehow worthwhile or that being on the dole unnecessarily is demeaning. It may be that he feels his client is made miserable by lack of self-respect. But it can also happen that he feels he ought to try to inject a connection between self-respect and work into someone whose self-respect at present depends more on a refusal to slave away to no advantage.

It might be asked what right social workers have to foist these values of autonomy and industry on clients who may not share them. The answer is complex. In some cases the social worker would be justified by reference to the interests, not of the client, but of society at large: there is only so much welfare money to go round, and those who can get on without it should therefore be encouraged to do so, even though the social worker's main *motivation* is the 'improvement' of his client. Similarly, since the social worker is himself a scarce and expensive resource, he is justified in trying to make one client less dependent on him so that he has more time for others.

But the wish to foster in a client a richer personal and social life cannot be justified in this way. We would submit, however, that if the social worker is *really* concerned about his client, he will inevitably think of his improvement as well as his happiness. We certainly care about the improvement of those we love best (for their sakes, that is), so part of a deep concern for someone is this element of wanting him to be the best that he can be; and it would moreover be patronizing for the social worker to think that the kind of life which he values most himself is somehow too good for clients. Restrictions are needed here, of course. First, the social worker must be sure that in judging his client to be in need of 'improvement' he is not failing to appreciate the qualities in the client's present mode of life. Second, he must be sure that the values he wishes to promote are reasonably uncontroversial ones, not private bees in the bonnet. Third, he must not *impose* on his client anything to which the client does not consent, unless he is clearly justified by the interests of third parties or by his statutory duties to society. We shall return to this last point in the next chapter.

We have spoken of social workers' efforts to foster independence, emotional and economic, and personal relationships. Do social workers have anything to do with the improvement of their clients' *moral* character? There are two types of case where this does seem at first sight to be the subject of their concern. The first is the case of children in 'moral danger', this being one of the situations which is held to justify social work departments in taking children away from their parents. At first sight it might seem that here the social worker must be acting in direct pursuit of the child's moral improvement. But this is less obvious when it is considered what kinds of situation are held to constitute moral danger: situations in which the child is involved, or likely to get involved, in sexual situations of various kinds: incest, prostitution, sexual assault. There is no feeling, or no comparable feeling, that children ought to be taken away from backgrounds which are delinquent in other ways. Presumably, then, the concern is not really for their *morals*, which are equally at stake in other kinds of delinquent home, but for their welfare in other senses. The hope which prompts their removal is to avoid or cut short the *emotional* damage such situations are thought to do to children, and this damage can be seen in terms either of straightforward unhappiness or in terms of stunted emotional development. (Whether such early experiences always do have these effects need not concern us, since the present point is that they are very widely believed to do so.) In this case, then, social workers are concerned, not with moral improvement, but with improvement in a vaguer sense or with happiness or both.

The other kind of case where the social worker appears to be concerned with moral improvement is that in which the probation officer attempts to instil into his client some notion of public-spiritedness and respect for the law: for example, in response to a client's claim that crime is perfectly satisfactory so long as one is not caught. But here one might ask what is the probation officer's purpose? Presumably he feels that the client's present attitude is all too likely to carry him back into crime, and that protestations that he will get caught are not going to be believed – or are not true in any case. His best hope of keeping his client out of crime, then, is to try to modify his attitude to the law and to society.

But why does he want to keep his client out of crime? If he is thinking only of his client's interests, he might do better in some cases to encourage his client to *commit* crime, but more dis-creetly. (For this reason, members of Children's Panels in Scotland, whose brief is to consider only the children's interests, sometimes find themselves, as law-abiding citizens, in a dilemma.) The answer surely is that, as a probation officer, he is *not* concerned solely with the client's interests; he is also employed to serve the good of society by trying to keep his client out of crime in cases where, in justice or in humanity, he cannot be put or cannot longer be kept in prison. It is society's welfare, then, not the client's moral welfare, which is his ultimate concern in preaching respect for law and public-spiritedness.

We do not wish to maintain that no social worker is ever con-cerned with his client's moral progress for its own sake. On the contrary; a religious social worker, for example, will presumably see his client as among other things a *soul* entrusted to his care. But the salvation of souls is a *personal* aim for some social workers, not an *intrinsic* aim of the social worker as such: as we saw, the two apparent examples of concern for moral welfare can readily be explained in terms of other more standard aims of social work.

The relationship between health and welfare

So far we have written as though health and welfare are entirely separate entities, one forming the aim of the doctor, the other of the social worker. But of course the situation is not as simple as this. There are many connections between health and welfare and hence between the aims of the professions. In this final section we wish to explore some of these.

First of all, health is clearly one very important *part* of welfare. As we saw earlier, health is a central part of a person's *interests*, in that it is reasonably wanted for its own sake and in that possession of it is a necessary condition for pursuing very many other goals. Part of the social worker's job, then, will be to promote the health of his client: to encourage him to seek medical advice and to take it, and to help him battle with, for example, inefficient National Health bureaucracy for free spectacles and the like. This is not of course to say that the social worker may usurp the doctor's function of bringing his unique skill to bear on the patient's medical problems. But the social worker has an *overall* responsibility for the patient which makes it quite reasonable that he should want to know what is going on medically. He will often also be the best person to *defend* the patient against the medical profession, where that is necessary; not where a *legal* defence is needed (for that he would have to call in another specialist!) but where what is needed is firm speaking by someone who has the confidence to address the doctor on equal terms as a fellow-professional: about, say, overpersuasion by the doctor to undergo some experimental or controversial treatment, or about a refusal to allow parents of young children to visit them in hospital.

We have said that the possession of health is a necessary condition for the pursuit of many other goals. The vital importance of this point for the social worker will be clear when it is remembered how often a person becomes a 'case' because he is unable to hold down a job through chronic ill-health, alcoholism or mental illness; the immediate problem may be his lack of financial means, but the underlying cause of the problem is a *medical* one, even if the client thinks of himself as a social-work rather than a medical case. It is often for such medical reasons, too, that a person (for example a neglectful parent or violent spouse) damages the interests of *others* to the extent that social workers become involved. In such cases the social worker needs to be able to consult the doctor on questions which are partly but not wholly medical: is this man sufficiently over his depression to be encouraged to look for a job? Is this woman likely to recover quickly from her mental illness and be able to look after her children again, or must long-term plans be made for them?

The second connection between health and welfare is of course the dependence of health, mental and physical, on other aspects of welfare, both material and non-material. To take an obvious example, an old person's health may be impaired because his home is damp, or up too many stairs, or because he cannot afford proper clothes, food or heating, or because he is not sufficiently able-bodied to look after himself. In all these situations, the expertise in specifying what is needed may be the doctor's, but the expertise in *getting* it, through statutory or voluntary services, is that of the social worker. And the skill required to thread the maze of regulations and to persuade officialdom of the urgency of need can be considerable. There are also, of course, cases where the dependence of health on welfare is at a deeper level, as in those cases of psychiatric or indeed physical illnesses which seem to be bound up with family or personal problems, and here the doctor may need social-work help not only in alleviating the problem but also in understanding it.

We hope it emerges from these fairly obvious considerations that health and welfare are inextricably bound up together and that the doctor and the social worker can each be – *must* each be – ancillary workers to the other, rather than mutually antagonistic, if these twin aims are to be achieved.

2 The principles governing the caring professions

Aims and rules

In the previous chapter we discussed the aims of the medical and the social work professions in terms of the two concepts of health and welfare. These were depicted, not only as the actual aims of the professions, but also as *values*, in two senses: they are liking values, things actually wanted for their own sakes, and ideal values, things which may be regarded as valuable, worthy of being wanted. We said that in so far as they are values, in both these senses, they are part of their possessor's *good*; and so those who subscribe to the value of *philanthropy*, concern for the good of others, will think it right, or a duty, to foster the health and welfare of others. The caring professions carry out this duty directly, in their work; the rest of us more indirectly, by contributing to rates and taxes and to charities.

The terminology of *values* is less common in philosophical writings than in writings on medicine and social work. But the doctrine which we expounded would be philosophically extremely familiar if translated into different terminology. It might be said that what we have discerned in the practice of the caring professions is a moral system of the kind which is called by philosophers 'ideal utilitarianism'. Ideal utilitarianism may be said to have two elements: the principle that right action is that which promotes as much good as possible for everyone (this corresponds to the value which we called 'philanthropy'), and the belief that this good is to be seen, partly no doubt in terms of what the people concerned want, but partly also in terms of *ideals* which are not simply reducible to what people want. Principles are narrower than values, being concerned only with what people should *do*, whereas values concern also feelings, wishes and attitudes. Apart from this narrowing, we may fairly say that the outlook which we ascribed in our previous chapter to the caring professions, taken in itself, is a kind of ideal utilitarianism, tending in some people towards pure hedonistic utilitarianism, the view that the only good is happiness or pleasure, or at any rate whatever people have as their liking values.

In fact utilitarianism, whether hedonistic or ideal, is not adequate by itself as an account of the underlying moral principles of the caring professions. The reasons for this are in the end the same as the reasons traditionally advanced for rejecting utilitarianism as an account of morality in general: we shall first sketch these in general terms and then show how they apply to the caring professions.

The first simple ideas in utilitarianism were that our sole duty is to produce as *much* good as possible and that good is to be seen simply as whatever people *want* ('pleasure' and/or 'happiness' are often used as a kind of shorthand for 'the objects of desire, whatever they may be'). The first difficulty is that this notion of good starts to seem inadequate to our convictions: surely, it is said, some things are more *worth* having than others, regardless of whether or how much people want them. This idea embodies not abandonment of utilitarian ideas but a shift from the earlier, hedonistic version to a more complex ideal utilitarianism. Second, the notion of *maximizing* good comes under fire, since it seems to sanction the possibility of grossly unequal *distributions* of good and so to conflict with basic intuitions of equity or fairness. Third, the basic notion of all forms of utilitarianism, that the sole criterion of the rightness of action is in terms of good *consequences* to be produced, comes under criticism: surely, it is often said, there are some kinds of action which are just *wrong*, or just *obligatory*, whether or not they produce the best consequences.

We shall now try to show how these criticisms of a general

utilitarian position, familiar to philosophers, can be made from
the narrower point of view of the caring professions. We have
already said in the foregoing chapter that members of these
professions are often interested in the improvement as well as in
the interests of their clients: this is one example of the idea that
some things are more worth having than others, independently of
people's wants. In this chapter and the next we shall look at some
of the moral rules and principles which seem to many medical
and social workers to set limits to the pursuit of the greatest good
of the greatest number and to govern the distribution of that
good. These principles can all be related to the notion, often
quoted in medical and social work circles, of respect for the
individual, his rights and claims, as we shall now try to demonstrate.

Respect for persons

We shall not argue for the principle of respect for the individual,
which is widely described as the central principle of the caring
professions.[1] We shall assume that medical and social workers do
in fact subscribe to some form of the principle of respect and
therefore try to regulate their pursuit of the *aims* of their
professions, as described in our previous chapter, by a regard for
the principle of respect. What we shall do briefly instead is to try
to say what it is in human beings which is respected or valued.

Since human beings alone are accorded this special worth by
those who subscribe to the principle of respect for the individual,
the answer must lie in those aspects of human beings which
importantly distinguish them from the rest of creation. There can
be considerable discussion as to what these are. But they certainly
include, as important ingredients, a capacity for self-determination
and a capacity for forming and pursuing ideal values. By 'self-
determination' we mean adopting ends and forming policies of
action to bring them about; self-determination thus goes beyond
the mere having of likes and dislikes (what we called 'liking
values'), though these will form its basis. In the capacity for
forming and pursuing ideals we would of course include the
capacity for *morality*, which for Kant was the essence of uniquely
human value; this Kantian doctrine is really a secularized version
of the Christian conception of man alone as made in God's image

and possessing a soul capable of salvation. But as we saw in the previous chapter, the realm of ideals extends beyond the scope of the moral.

It will be noted that we have not mentioned either the exercise of theoretical reason or the possession of emotions. This is because these features, in so far as they are characteristically human, are already included in self-determination. The working out of problems, however abstract, is done at the behest of the *practical* reason – there is an *end* in view, even if it is only the satisfaction of curiosity; that which can work out theoretical problems without a purpose of its own is not a man but a computer. Again, emotions either involve purposes and plans – for example, fear involves plans to escape or defend oneself – or they are at the instinctive level of an animal.

One problem which arises from any attempt to isolate the common features which constitute the unique worth of human beings (what may be called their 'distinctive endowment')[2] is that the very attempt seems to undermine the stress on individuality which prompted it. If there is some feature or features of human beings which make them worthwhile, does it not follow that what we value is *not* individual human beings but humanity in the abstract, which can be exemplified equally well whoever the exemplar is? Now Kant does sometimes write as though humanity in the abstract were what is valuable. But the very nature of self-determination and the formation of ideals guarantees the centrality of the individual, since the capacity for choice and commitment is in a sense a capacity for individuality, for making one's own decisions and plans, ungoverned by anything else. All the same, this apparent difficulty does make it clear that what is valuable in human beings is not merely their possessing this capacity, which *is* in a sense common property, but their individual *exercise* of it.

A second difficulty is more serious. We have spoken of respect for human beings, and then given an account of what we respect in human beings in terms of self-determination and the formation of ideals. But not all human beings possess these attributes. It is not meaningful to attribute a capacity for self-determination, in the relevant sense, to infants, the severely subnormal, the severely mentally ill, the senile, and those in a terminal coma. But we regard such people as worthy of respect. These attributes then, it might seem, cannot after all be the object of our respect.

We can begin to meet this difficulty if we call into question one of the premises of the foregoing argument. It is not true that we think these categories of people are due *all* the respect accorded to normal adults. For example, we do not feel we should accede to the wishes of a senile person or a small child where these are likely to do harm to him, or that we have a duty to consult him as to his welfare. Again, we do not necessarily think we should – indeed, we often *cannot* – make sure that a mentally ill person understands his situation or allow him to decide his future. This is of course a matter of degree, but it would be reasonable to say that in extreme cases those without the distinctive endowment of a human being are not given the special respect generally thought due to a fellow human being.

Does it follow that such people are regarded rather as like animals, to be treated with kindness and compassion, but not thought valuable in themselves? This is not the case either, as can be seen if one considers what is tolerated for animals but not for men of any kind. Leaving aside the questions of using animals for food and for experimentation, one may simply consider the question of transplant organs. If there is a chance that an organ from an ape, say, might do for a man, a doctor will not hesitate to kill the ape. But no one would kill a mental defective for transplant material, even if it were certain that his organs could save several people.[3]

It appears, then, that we acknowledge *three* levels of concern. On the lowest level are the animals, who are regarded as having a presumptive right not to suffer. (Whether even this minimal right is respected in practice is another matter.) Next we have what we may call 'sub-normal' humans, who are not accorded full respect but are not treated like animals either. (Again, they sometimes *are*, in practice – 'they are treated no better than animals' is a frequent criticism of mental hospitals.) Finally we have the normal humans who are accorded full respect. We may describe the distinction between the sub-normal and normal human beings by employing the evaluative concept of a *person* to mark off those human beings who are worthy of full respect for the individual. The word 'person' is often used in ordinary speech in this evaluative way: thus we say of a senile old man that he is no longer a *person*: 'There isn't a person there any more', or we say of someone severely mentally ill, 'You can't at present regard him as a person at all', or we say of an infant, 'He's not really a *person* yet'. We shall always use the word in this way, as a technical term for a human being worthy of full respect as an individual.

The distinction between our attitudes to persons and our attitudes to other human beings allows us to maintain that the 'distinctive endowment' of a human being is central to respect for individuals, while acknowledging that not all human beings possess this endowment. But on this argument it is not clear why we should treat humans who are not persons better than we treat animals. The answer has to be in terms of our sense of kinship with others of the same species. Whether this is a *justification*, or just a biological *explanation*, is another question.

We have developed, then, an idea of respect for the individual person as a basic principle in terms of which the objectives of the caring professions have to be pursued. It is not clear as yet what is entailed by respect for persons; nevertheless we can derive various more specific principles from the notion of respect for persons by means of a consideration of the distinctive human endowment in its various aspects and of the conditions needed to make it flourish; or, to put the same point another way, we can distinguish the various *rights* against others which a person has in virtue of his right to be respected as a person. For rights and obligations are opposite sides of the same coin: if there is a duty to treat people in a certain way they thereby have a right to be so treated.

One of these basic rights is the right to life itself. Clearly, if we set an ultimate value on the individual exercise of certain attributes characteristic of a person, we have to respect the life without which such exercise cannot take place. As we shall see, however, the idea of a 'right to life' has to be considered in the context of a wider discussion of the importance of the preservation of human life.

The right to life

In the previous chapter we discussed the doctor's aims in terms of the curing of illness and promotion of health. But many people would say that his paramount aim is the saving of human *life*. This statement obviously needs some refinement: for one thing, a doctor can get into a situation where he must in effect *destroy* one life to save another. But broadly speaking the common view is that the preservation of life is a central part of a doctor's work, and this view may be expressed even more strongly in terms of a solemn duty not to kill anyone or let him die when he could be saved, however good the reasons may be. In many cases, of course, no moral or philosophical problem arises with regard to this doctrine. But difficult cases, such as abortion, euthanasia and the removal of life-support systems from comatose patients, raise the question of the basis of the doctrine of the special importance of life.

As might be expected, the two types of argument advanced for according this significance to human life stress either the *wants* of the individual whose life it is, or some ideal in terms of which human life can be shown to have a special value. Thus, appeal can be made either to interests, or to the sanctity of human life and the immeasurable worth of human beings conceived as ends-in-themselves. These two lines of thought do not always yield the same answers concerning the borderline cases, as we shall see.

A crude form of the appeal to *wants* is the proposition that life is supremely important because people want above all to stay alive; or, even if they do not think about staying alive as such, they would desperately want to if life were threatened. Moreover, being alive is a necessary condition for their achieving the vast majority of the other things they want (not *everything* they want, because presumably wants which are expressed in a will can only be fulfilled when the wanter is dead). If these are the reasons for fostering someone's life, then someone who is in a permanently comatose state, who is not and will never be in a position to want anything, has no claim to have his life respected. Again, a person who does not want to live may on this view be allowed to die – or indeed helped to die, if he cannot manage to procure his own death. But since there is no way of reversing this action once taken, it is reasonable and in keeping with the appeal to wants to make sure that the person who 'wants to die' *really* wants to do so, i.e. has a firm and settled purpose and not a sudden mood of depression which would pass away leaving him content to live.

The appeal to wants, then, licenses what may be called 'voluntary euthanasia', but forbids involuntary euthanasia, the killing or letting die of someone who wants to go on living. But this restriction is hard to interpret in practice. It might be objected, for example, that it seems to allow us to kill off the senile or mentally deficient, since they cannot meaningfully be said to want anything so abstract. But this is too sweeping. Such people can certainly be said to be capable of enjoying life or of looking forward to treats promised in the future (though they may not understand what is meant by 'next month'), and this is surely enough to say that they want to live. This may be granted, but it might then be said that small babies cannot be said either to want to live or to want, as distinct from instinctively seek, anything else; and no one supposes that we are at liberty to get rid of them when convenient. Here, presumably, the principle of respecting people's desire to live has to be *refined* to include respecting the lives of those who *will* in the future, as far as we know, develop the normal desire to live, together with the capacity for forming desires and projects in general.

This refinement referring to people's expected future wants has other implications, for example, with regard to abortion. From the point of view of expected future wants the foetus is in the same position as the small baby; so, where there is no more reason to expect other than the normal desires to be acquired later, there is no more reason to suppose that killing a foetus is justified than to suppose that killing a baby is. But there might be two types of case where what we have called the normal wants cannot be expected: where the foetus is so *severely* deficient mentally that future wants cannot be attributed to it; and where it is so severely handicapped that in all probability it will come to wish it were dead. If these two cases could be detected *in utero* they would, if we appeal to the wants principle, provide grounds for justifying abortion. The difficulty in practice, however, would be to *identify* instances of the second type of case – it will be noticed that we provide no example of the kind of handicap. Most people have on occasion said to themselves, 'If I were in X's shoes I'd commit suicide' although X is apparently content and even happy. In any case, happiness is not exactly the point. Many people who are unhappy can feel that life is worth living. These facts make it almost impossible to say with certainty that a given foetus or baby, were it to survive, would regret being alive.

The same considerations apply to the possible case of a person who does not want to die at present but who will come later to think that it would have been better to have died earlier. Jonathan Glover imagines one such case: he says that if he had been a Jew in Nazi Germany who thought that his family did not understand the full horror of what they were to undergo he might well have felt justified in killing them and himself, on the ground that this is what they would want if they really understood.[4] One can imagine a doctor in Nazi Germany, or in Soviet Russia today, faced with a similar dilemma. It is impossible not to feel sympathy with Glover's reaction, but difficult to justify it solely on the grounds he puts forward: can one ever be sure what people would want or what they don't understand? The feeling that it might in such circumstances be right to kill someone rests partly on an appeal, not to what they do or might want, but to a judgment (which they may not share) about what kinds of life and death are dignified, fitting and suitable rather than degrading and undignified.

It will be noted that the very limited licence for abortion given by the appeal to wants draws a distinction, not between the foetus and the baby once born, but between the creature, whether foetus or baby, which can expect to want to be alive and the creature which cannot. It is, however, the distinction between foetus and baby which is seen as vitally important by many people, who support widespread abortion but would regard the killing of a baby for similar reasons as indefensible. They regard a baby as a person in his own right, so to speak, whereas the foetus is simply part of his mother to be disposed of as she wishes.

It is hard to base an argument on this sharp division between foetus and baby, especially since it grows more and more artificial with the prevalence of induced labour and the increase in techniques for preserving very premature babies. But the line of thinking of those whom we may for simplicity call the pro-abortionists points to an important deficiency in the appeal-to-wants arguments as so far presented. We have spoken as though the wants only of the person whose life is in question come into the calculation. But, as the pro-abortionists make clear, the death of one creature can be strongly desired by someone else. If we make the obligation to respect someone's life rest only on his *desire* to live, might not the importance of this desire be outweighed by other people's desires, stronger or more numerous, for his death? In other words, might not someone be justified, on this basis, in thinking, 'All right, Granny, you don't want to die. But what's so special about *your* wants? If it's a matter of *wants*, we've got force of numbers on our side: *I* want you to die, and Tom wants you to die, and Dick wants you to die, and Harry wants you to die...' No one thinks this argument is justified, although it seems to be a corollary of the appeal to wants; that type of appeal therefore stands in need of further refinement.

The refinement needed is in terms of the idea of a *right*. People are said to have a *right* to life, and this means that others have an obligation, not merely to weigh one person's desire to live against all the other desires that people may have, but to give this particular desire paramount importance. The person whose right it is may perhaps *waive* that right, but unless he does so his life cannot be weighed against other people's mere desires. Nor can we say without qualification even that other people's *rights* can be weighed against the right to life: after all, a son or daughter looking after an impossible elderly parent can say, 'I've a right to some fun while I'm young', but no one thinks that this kind of right can plausibly be set against a right to *life*. The right to life is so basic that it must be respected *first*, before other so-called rights come into the picture at all.

The assertion of a 'right to life' does not entail the simple assertion that it is always wrong to take a life. There are situations where, on any natural view of the case, the doctor must choose between the life of a foetus and that of a mother. Again, there might be a situation where taking one life saves many others: a 'right to life' doctrine would not entail that Hitler's doctor had to respect Hitler's life rather than that of millions of Jews, even taking into account the trust a patient has to have in his doctor. Nor does a right to life entail that doctors must always attempt to preserve life in preference to other tasks: we do not say that *all* resources should go into kidney machines and other life-saving devices in preference to clinics concerned with non-fatal illness; *some* balance between the life of one and the benefits of others is clearly accepted. But the 'right to life' entails a prohibition of killing someone simply to please others, and a weighting of resources and time in favour of saving life.

We have depicted the right to life as something which depends on people's *wish* to live, either explicit, or implicit in their wish to do things and get things in the future. If the right is seen in this way, it is regarded as something which can be *waived*: if it depends on its possessor's wishes, it can clearly be discarded at will. But there are difficulties about regarding the right to life as based solely on wishes in this way. The first difficulty is that if such a right is simply a specially important want, it is not really clear *why* it should have the paramount status which it does; it would seem that a right which is in the last analysis a matter of a person's wants should logically be overruled if there is a sufficiently large weight of wants on the other side. The second difficulty is that some people have a sense that life is not a thing which a person may lay down at will, and this idea cannot be accommodated in terms of a doctrine which construes rights in terms of wants.

There is, however, another way in which the right to life can be seen: as a recognition of the special *worth* or *value* in human life, a value which is independent of its possessor's wanting it. Seen in this way, the right to life lays an *obligation* on the possessor, no less than on others, to cherish this thing of value; he will not be entitled to waive his right to life since life has a value independent of his wishes, and others will not be entitled to take his life even in accordance with his wishes, since the obligation to respect it does not depend in any case on his wishes. (For a parallel case, consider the right to *liberty*: it is often maintained that a man is not morally permitted to throw away his own liberty, i.e. that this too is not a right which depends on its possessor *wanting* to keep it.)

But there are problems about according a special status to human life, as we saw in the previous section. If we say that human beings are worthy of a special respect, then we must say what it is about them which makes them worthy of this respect; we suggested their capacity for self-determination and for the adoption of ideals. But many creatures who are biologically speaking human beings do not possess these capacities: for example, the severely mentally handicapped, the senile, those in an irreversible coma. If we base the right to life on the unique value of the human being, it seems to follow that these people do not have a right to life.

It might be maintained here that a Christian view of man does give some reason to respect the lives of *all* men as men, because they are seen as having an immortal soul which is conceived of as somehow independent of temporal accidents, such as mental deficiency; from the point of view of *soul-hood*, the idiot is to be seen as no worse off than anyone else.

This doctrine is not only very obscure in itself, it leaves the basic problem untouched. For if what is precious about human beings is their immortal *souls*, why should a special importance be set on preserving their mortal *lives*? Why should the Christian not take the view that it is sometimes an act of charity to send an afflicted soul to its Maker – not, perhaps, if it is the soul of a person yet capable of acquiring truer repentance and greater purity, but if it is the soul of one to whom these ideas cannot even be applied? The Christian doctor cannot answer this question by saying it is wrong to interfere with God's plan, for if God's plan simply means what would happen without the doctor's interference, it would then always be wrong to save the life of someone who would otherwise die. The doctor has to maintain instead that it is God's will that human life – the life of *anyone* of the human species – be regarded as sacred, and that this is simply a basic command to be taken on trust.

The non-Christian, however, or the Christian who takes the view that God's will is whatever can be assumed to be reasonable on other grounds, can take a more discriminating view of the intrinsic value of human life. If he takes each case on its merits he will say that those who are utterly incapable of rationality or morality, who are, in other words, incapable of a characteristically *human* life, do not possess lives of intrinsic value. On the other hand, he would say that someone who is suffering intensely is no less human on that account and indeed may be going through experiences of immense spiritual importance constituting one of the peaks of human life.

This kind of doctrine, if left unmodified by other considerations, would imply that euthanasia of the severely mentally subnormal and incurably insane or abortion of severely deficient foetuses (not of those who are not far below human status) is permissible, whereas euthanasia or abortion of someone who was or would be *miserable* and who wanted or would want to die, would not be, provided he was capable of human thought. But this conclusion suggests a much more clear-cut and ruthless policy than actually obtains even among those who hold a secularized version of the 'intrinsic value of human life' view.

This difference in practice comes about for several reasons. One reason is that the view may be modified by considerations about what people want; for, even if a doctor himself holds that human life is sacred, he may also feel that he should not force the consequences of this view on a terminally ill and suffering patient who asks to be put out of his misery, or an expectant mother who thinks it wrong to bear a child which may suffer wretchedly as a result of *spina bifida*.

A second reason is that those who hold that human life is intrinsically valuable tend to refuse to consider each *individual's* claim to humanity, and behave as though the human *species* as a whole is worthy of respect because of its special characteristics, even though these characteristics are not possessed by all members of the species. In other words, those human beings who are not capable of self-determination and the adoption of ideals are nevertheless given the courtesy title of 'human'. This extension of respect is not strictly rational, though it may be a likeable and attractive sort of irrationality, and in any case is probably ineradicable, the result of a biologically determined sense of kinship with other members of one's biological species – ineradicable, that is, as far as feelings go, for most people will agree that there are some extreme cases where it is right to overcome the repugnance against taking the life of a creature of human stock.

We have, then, two basic principles in terms of which medical workers can see their duty to respect and foster human life. One is based on the presumed or actual wish of human beings to live, and this principle would permit the euthanasia or abortion of those who have or will have a life so wretched that they want to end it and of those who are unable and will never be able to have any wants constituting desire for or enjoyment of life. The other principle is based on a sense of the intrinsic value of characteristically human life and would of itself permit euthanasia or abortion only of life which could be described as subhuman, though respect for people's wishes and a kind of *extension* of respect to all of human stock might modify this in practice.

It will doubtless now be retorted that no doctor or nurse holds that euthanasia, at any rate, is justified on the scale that either of these principles suggests; if they did, there would be no cabbage-like imbeciles in institutions or patients in irreversible coma kept alive by machines. In fact, however, doctors support at least as wide a range of euthanasia, but by *omission* only, not by commission. For example, if an imbecile baby fails to breathe properly at birth they may omit to resuscitate it, hoping it will die; they refrain from operating on a baby with severe *spina bifida*, on the ground that this will only prolong a life which will be wretched; they decide in advance that certain patients who are, for example, senile, incontinent and in pain are not to be resuscitated if they suffer a cardiac arrest. Such doctors are not *killing* their patients; but they are letting them die when they might save them, for reasons which clearly relate to one or other of those we have mentioned.

It will still be said that these examples go no way towards showing that the medical profession condones euthanasia on the scale our principles suggest, since there is a vast difference between killing someone and letting him die. Now there is certainly a *difference*, but it is not clear that this difference can make it wrong to *do* what it would be permissible, or perhaps obligatory, to *allow* by deliberate omission.

Let us consider this point a little further. General medical opinion thinks it right to omit to make a grossly deformed newborn baby breathe, but wrong to smother it if it breathes by itself. What is the difference between the two cases? In both, the *motive* is the same – pity for the future sufferings of the baby and its family. In both, the *result* is the same – the death of the baby. In both, the result is brought about by a deliberate *decision* – for since normal practice is to get new babies breathing, there has to be a deliberate decision not to do so in a given case. It is true that the decision not to stimulate breathing is not *premeditated*. But some such decisions *are* more or less premeditated, as when a doctor says to a nurse, 'Next time he has a cardiac arrest, don't revive him.' Again, the tendency is to feel that somehow one is less *responsible* for omissions than for actions. But, as we have seen, the omissions in question are the outcome of decisions, sometimes premeditated ones, not to do what would normally be one's duty. It is difficult therefore to escape responsibility for them.

The only point of difference remaining seems to be that the act involves intervention in the natural course of events, whereas the omission involves letting events take their course. What *moral* difference does this make? Doctors certainly do not hold it to be wrong in general to interfere with the natural course of events when this will be beneficial. It will often be said that we should respect the workings of Nature or of Providence and leave well alone. But then this suggestion gives rise to a dilemma: either *whatever* happens naturally is to be regarded as the workings of Nature or Providence, in which case *any* medical intervention is unjustified; or whatever happens naturally *and is for the best* is the working of Nature or Providence, in which case respect for Nature or Providence does not forbid us to interfere with the natural course of events when it is *not* for the best.

The strategy of these last arguments has been to try to break down the sharp moral distinction which doctors' practice draws between killing patients and letting them die. If the breakdown of the distinction is accepted, there are two possibilities. Doctors can hang on to a precept that 'Thou shalt not kill' and so conclude that they are wrong sometimes to omit to keep alive. Or, if they are sure that these omissions are sometimes right and indeed a duty, they can acknowledge that it follows that it would sometimes be right to kill a patient.

It is the latter conclusion to which this section points. We have discussed two criteria, either of which will sometimes give rise to such cases, though the criteria would not give the same answer in all difficult examples. Which criterion to adopt, or if both, how to weight them, is something which has to be left to individual moral judgment. Clearly, however, one important factor points to the need for every restraint: there is no way of reversing the decision to kill a patient once it has been acted upon.

We said earlier that the capacity for self-determination, for forming and carrying out one's own plans and policies, is an important part of the distinctive human endowment. The next right which we shall discuss relates to this capacity. For if the capacity for self-determination is worthy of respect in itself, it follows that people ought, as far as possible, to be allowed to pursue their own plans without interference, both because they exercise their distinctive humanity thereby and also because too little scope for choice weakens the capacity itself and makes the human being less of a person.

The right to liberty

The phrase 'the right to liberty' in some contexts sounds like the right not to be enslaved: 'we hold these rights to be self-evident ... life, liberty and the pursuit of happiness'.[5] But here we are referring to a wider right, the right to *be allowed* to act as one chooses. The duty corresponding to this right is a duty not to *do* something but to *refrain* from preventing another person from doing as he chooses.

No one has the unlimited right to do as he chooses. Such a right would be self-contradictory, as the things which people choose to do often conflict: if A is allowed to do whatever he chooses, he may well thereby prevent B from doing whatever *he* chooses. Moreover what A chooses to do may harm B's interests, even where it does not interfere with his choices. Again, in a complex and interdependent community, A must be made to do some things which he would not choose to do (such as pay taxes) in order to bring about large-scale schemes from which everyone benefits, including A. But the presumption remains in favour of A's liberty, and curtailment of that liberty is regarded as justified only for the sake of others' liberty or others' interests or the general good. Otherwise A has a right not to be prevented from acting, either by the law or by private individuals.

The great classic source of this principle of liberty is J.S. Mill's essay *On Liberty*:

> the sole end for which mankind are warranted, individually or collectively, in interfering with the liberty of action of any of their number is self-protection. His own good, either physical or moral, is not a sufficient warrant.[6]

Mill's reference to self-protection means that it is legitimate to forbid a person to perform certain actions only if it can be shown that his performance of them will interfere with the liberty of others, or will in some way harm their interests. It is important to note that the principle of liberty forbids interference with someone even *for his own good*. This is partly because outsiders have no reason to suppose that they know best; but also because a man's own exercise of choice, his government of his own life, is in itself a good in terms of the distinctive endowment of a human being; a good which other people remove if they *make* him do things, however well-meaning their motive.

We can illustrate the right to liberty with reference to our subject-matter, by suggesting that a consequence of it is that in certain circumstances people have a right to be unhealthy. Now it is not true of *all* types of unhealth that there is a *legal* right to be unhealthy. That is, while the law does not condemn unhealth as such, it does say that for certain sorts, for example, certain sorts of infectious disease, it is not legally permissible to be in this unhealthy state and to act as if one were not unhealthy, i.e. to mix freely with other people. Why does the law single out this sort of unhealth and say that one has no unqualified right to remain in it untreated? The answer is obviously that in this state one is liable to harm others. And this answer gives us the criterion which can be used not only in legal but also in non-legal situations: there is a moral (and legal) right to be unhealthy so long as one is not harming others by one's unhealth.

For an example of the right to be unhealthy which brings out the fact that this right constitutes a duty of non-interference on others' part, consider the issue of fluoridization. In this context someone might assert the right to be unhealthy. He would here be saying that others have a duty not to interfere with his choice as to whether or not he wants this sort of medication. Some opponents of the fluoridization of the water supply appeal to a right of this sort. In this case the evidence seemed to suggest that the overwhelming benefit to everyone should have moral priority over the assertion by a minority of their right. But the assertion of the right made perfectly good logical sense, and there could be cases in which priority should go to those individuals who would prefer to be unhealthy rather than agree to certain forms of medication.

Another sphere in which a person may defend his liberty by claiming a right to be unhealthy is that of mental health. As we have seen, the whole idea of mental health is a difficult one; whereas with physical unhealth there are objective features – abnormal biochemistry, malignant growth, etc. – which are causally connected with the subjective *feeling* of ill-health, there *need* not be any such causal correlation between deviant behaviour patterns and physical causation. Moreover, whereas in the case of physical ill-health there are widely agreed criteria for what are or are not unhealthy states of the physical organism, the criteria for what is or is not deviant behaviour are essentially contestable. In this context there is therefore a danger of labelling, as mentally ill, behaviour which is deviant only in the statistical non-evaluative sense that it is different from what most people in a given social group in fact do. To assert a right to be 'mentally unhealthy' in such a context need not be anything other than asserting a right to mind one's own business.

To say that a person has a right to be unhealthy, then, is to say that no medical or social worker or other person may compel him against his wishes to take any steps to protect or improve his health. This right is formally safeguarded in many ways: for example, a person may discharge himself from hospital, he has to sign a form consenting to an operation, etc. But as we have seen, this liberty applies only to those aspects of health which affect only the person himself. The criterion for justified interference permits (at any rate morally permits, though the law would not always in practice permit) interference for the protection of others.

The criterion, as we have formulated it in the context of health, is however open to two sorts of objection, a more and a less radical sort. Let us look first at the less radical sort. This objection has several forms but the common element is that it concedes the general validity of the criterion but points out that, certainly as far as moral rights are concerned, the criterion establishes considerably less freedom than at first seems to be the case. The first form in which this less radical objection can be stated turns on two premises, or sets of premises, each of which seems to be valid. The first of these is concerned with the nature of social life, which involves people living in close proximity one with another. The second premise or set of premises concerns some common ways in which diseases are transmitted, via infection or contagion. Now granted these two premises, it would seem that a large number of common diseases, such as 'the common cold', are likely to cause harm to others. It would therefore follow from the criterion that we do not have an unqualified right to be unhealthy in a large number of common ways.

There could be a second form of the less radical objection. This argument depends on the premise that medical service is a scarce commodity, such that there is not enough to go round for all who need it. Granted the premise we can then assert that those who claim the right to be unhealthy are in effect claiming the right to act in ways which will endanger or damage their health, knowing that in the event of their serious ill-health they can have access to medical services on an equal footing with those who through no fault of their own have become ill. But to act in this way is indirectly to injure others since it is to create avoidable demands on scarce resources.

A third form of the argument is a more general one. It turns on the premise that the vast majority of people play some part in the division of labour and make a contribution to society. In other words, it is true, and indeed necessarily true, that citizens have social duties; and most people are citizens. But we cannot perform our duties to others without health. How then can there be a right to be unhealthy?

These three arguments cast some doubt on the conception of a right to be unhealthy, or at least suggest its limited scope. The arguments do not in any way question the validity of the principle that we have a right to do or be that which will not harm others, but they suggest that the occasions on which our ill-health may harm others are more numerous than may at first appear.

The more radical objection to an alleged right to be unhealthy challenges the assumption that we have this right even in those limited cases where our ill-health harms no one else. On the more radical view, harm to *others* is not the only consideration; it is wrong in *itself* to be unhealthy. An argument of this radical sort could be based on religious assumptions of the kind we mentioned when discussing health as an ideal, but there can also be secular forms of the radical argument. One form might begin by asserting that we all recognize a duty to develop or realize our gifts, and then go on to claim that health is a necessary condition of this. There could not therefore be a moral right to that which would block this process of self-realization. This argument is not convincing, however, since it requires a premise of doubtful validity – that the possession of health is a necessary condition of self-realization. History seems to be against this premise. Many people – not just the great, like Beethoven or Emily Brontë – have realized their gifts despite ill-health. Indeed, it is possible to claim in some cases that it was *because* of their ill-health that some people have turned to pursuits which brought out their intellectual, artistic or moral gifts. A more plausible secular approach is that mentioned earlier: to regard a person as a mind/body unity and to say that it is incumbent on us to make our human natures flourish. It follows from this approach to the moral life that there

could be no right to be unhealthy, but rather there is a duty to
preserve one's health as one aspect of one's total well-being. And
to maintain this claim is not to deny the point that sometimes ill-
health will *in fact* produce the conditions which lead to great
achievement.

We therefore have two possible approaches to the idea of a right
to be unhealthy. There is the approach of liberal morality, which
allows the existence of such a right as one aspect of the liberty of
the individual, however restricted in practice the scope of that
right may be by the effect of one's ill-health on others. On the
other hand, there are traditions of moral thinking, religious and
secular, which would deny the existence of such a right. It might
at first seem that there is no way of reconciling these two points of
view; and this would be unfortunate, since the approach of liberal
morality springs from the principle of respect for the individual
endorsed by practitioners of the caring professions, while the
notion of health as a value in its own right is almost equally well
embedded in our tradition of thought. But this conflict is only
apparent, as the right which one side maintains is not the same
right as that which the other side denies.

This can be seen if we recall again that the right which J.S. Mill
was keen to maintain was a right to *non-interference*, a right
against others who thereby have a duty to leave one alone. It is
one case of what is called a right of *recipience*: a right to be treated
in a certain way.[7] But to say that someone has a right to non-
interference with respect to certain conduct is *not* necessarily to
say that the conduct is morally acceptable or permissible. In other
words, a person can sometimes have a right to do what is wrong.
Mill makes clear that he envisages this possibility when he says:
'His own good, either physical *or moral*, is not a sufficient
warrant [for interference]'[8] (though Mill is not always consistent
on this point). Of course, many people would maintain that
conduct cannot be said to be wrong unless it affects others, in
which case it is liable to interference in any case. But it is perfectly possible to maintain that there is a realm of conduct which
does not affect others and which is therefore one's own business
as far as interference goes but which may be subject to moral
appraisal.

Now the party which claims that we have a duty to maintain
health even where others are not affected can perfectly consistently

allow that people have a right not to be coerced to be healthy. The right that this party wishes to deny is of a different kind, and is what we may call a right of *action*, in contrast to a right of recipience. A right of action concerns not other people's duties towards the possessor of the right, but the possessor's own duty, or rather absence of duty: to have a right of action to do something is to be under no obligation to do otherwise. Those who maintain that health is itself a good are denying this kind of right to be unhealthy and saying that on the contrary we do have an obligation to maintain health. (It need not however be seen as an *overriding* obligation; a person who subscribed in general to this point of view might nevertheless think it his duty to undertake some service in a swampy region of the world where his health is likely to be seriously impaired.)

As will be clear from the foregoing chapter, we would maintain that there is an obligation to maintain health. But we would also maintain that a person has a right (a right of recipience) to remain unhealthy where others are not affected. As we have seen, this right is to some extent a legal right; that is to say, coercion is forbidden by law. But even where the law does not protect the individual, he has a moral right to be free from undue pressure and bullying to undergo treatment which he does not want. This is an important liberty.

It does not follow, however, that wherever a person's ill-health affects others, medical workers have the right to interfere. In extreme cases, of course, the law steps in and insists for example that a person be isolated if he suffers from infectious disease. But there is an enormous range of cases, in health as in other aspects of life, where the law allows people to do things injurious to others without taking action. This is partly because the law has to be general and the degree to which a person's ill-health affects others depends on his particular circumstances; partly because the law can take note only of major injuries to others (*de minimis non curat lex*); partly because of difficulties in some cases of *proving* that ill-health was the case of the damage to others and that it was avoidable. Where the law is silent, may the medical worker speak? For instance, may a doctor castigate someone who is ruining his health by over-eating or over-drinking, and who is as a result making his dependants suffer? Again, should he refuse to sign certificates for those whose illness is their own fault and who are therefore defrauding the taxpayer in claiming benefit?

The answer, we submit, is different in the two types of case. As a possible signer of certificates for benefit, a doctor has a kind of official role as agent for the State. This might be thought to entitle him to look after the State's interest; but by the same token, he is entitled to interfere only to the degree that he is authorized by the State. If the State does not *ask* whether the illness in question is partly self-induced, the State presumably does not wish to undertake the difficult task of discriminating between those cases where it is and those where it is not. As a possible castigator, however, he is no one's agent. Nor is he in a special position *qua* doctor, except in so far as his medical knowledge may enable him to realize, as others do not, that a particular person can be blamed for his ill-health because it is partly produced or partly prolonged by his own actions or omissions. The doctor's situation is therefore comparable to that of anyone else who finds out that an acquaintance is treating a spouse or child badly, and, believing that he alone knows this, wonders whether to 'say anything' to the wrongdoer. Opinions would differ on this, but a common assumption would be that a person has *no* right (of action) to interfere or reprove unless either the harm being done is fairly extreme or he is a friend of or in some other special relationship to the wrongdoer.

Two consequences would arise from this *laissez-faire* attitude to others' wrongdoing to third parties. One is that, in general, a doctor who says 'You oughtn't to smoke and give yourself bronchitis – it's not fair on your wife' may be being as officious as a bank manager who says, 'You oughtn't to gamble and run up overdrafts – it's not fair on your wife'. If it does not seem so at first, this is for one of two reasons: either because we are apt to regard doctors, without warrant, as moral authorities; or because we see them as standing in some kind of personal relationship to patients (see chapter 3). The other consequence is that Mill's distinction between the sphere in which a man is immune from interference and the sphere in which he is liable to it turns out to be less important than one might suppose, since in practice we seem to disapprove also of those who interfere in many situations in which Mill's criterion *would* allow interference. Perhaps the Victorians were more tolerant of unrelated moral agents uttering reproofs to each other than we should now be.

The principle of respect for liberty is as important in social work as in medicine: no one may be coerced, even for his own good, into behaving in ways which affect no one but himself. But there are aspects of social work in which people have to be coerced for *others'* good. An obvious example is the care of children. A person has a right to live in squalid filthy conditions himself and to fail to eat properly. But he has no right to impose this life on his children, and social workers are regarded as justified in intervening to protect children. (This is, of course, true with regard to health also; for example, Jehovah's Witnesses are allowed to refuse blood transfusions for themselves, but not normally for their children.) Again, prison officers and probation officers may make people do things for the good of society, not for their own good.

This last point needs a little explanation. Of course these workers, like any other social workers, can care about their clients and try to help them. But either the help must be sought or at least welcomed by the client, or it must be justifiable in terms of good to others. For example, a prisoner who is made to learn a trade will be less likely to return to crime; a probationer who is forbidden to go to the football matches where he committed his original crime will thereby be kept out of trouble. If a social worker steps outside those limits, and tries to make a client do something 'for his own good', he is encroaching on his client's liberty. Of course the distinction is not always easy to draw between suggestion and encouragement on the one hand and coercion on the other. It would seem, however, that a social worker who used his discretionary powers with regard to various benefits to bribe or threaten clients into behaviour which *he* approved of, but which has no clear relevance to society's interests, is going beyond what is acceptable. It must also be remembered that what is merely suggestion to a strong, independent character can have the force of coercion to a weak or dependent one.

We have depicted the individual's right to liberty as based on the value of his capacity as a person to choose for himself. It follows that the right exists only in a modified form in those cases where personhood is incomplete: in the case of young children, for example, or in the case of mental deficiency. In such cases medical and social workers do feel themselves to be justified in some degree of interference in a person's liberty. For example, an insane person can be certified if he is a danger to *himself*, as well as if he is a danger to others; but the restrictions on liberty have to be proportionate to the limitations in personhood, and no one is justified in interfering with another simply on the ground that he '*knows* better'. He doubtless should explain what he knows as far as he can, to help his client to make an informed choice. But liberty includes the right to make one's own mistakes.

The right to know the truth

Under this heading we are going to discuss, not the research worker's commitment to discovering and publishing the truth, but the duty of the caring worker to *tell* the truth to his clients about their situation. This duty, as we shall see, connects in important ways with respect for the clients' capacity for self-determination. It is relevant both to medical and to social work, although the problems will vary to some extent because of the different natures of the doctor's and the social worker's jobs. It should also be noted that sometimes humane decisions on what and how much to say may require co-operation between the medical and the social worker.

At first sight the issues which raise questions about the caring worker's duty to tell the truth seem to fall into three distinct categories. First of all, there is the question whether to tell a patient or client the painful truth about his *situation*: that he is not likely to live, that he is going to remain bed-ridden, or that he is going to be evicted from his house. In this same category we could place cases of telling parents about the situation of a child, especially the case of mental handicaps. Secondly, there is the question of telling patients about the possible dangers of proposed treatments or procedures. Thirdly, there are problems connected with *trials* of drugs or treatments. Some of these problems are covered by the second category, but there are also situations where what is involved is not a question of *danger*, but of concealing from a patient whether he is receiving the old drug or the new, the drug or the placebo, and so on. The first two categories can be marked off from the third in that the third seems to involve deception intrinsically (either there is deception or the trial cannot take place) whereas the other two cases seem to offer a choice between deception and non-deception which is quite distinct from the medical decisions about what steps to take. Again, the first type of case differs from the second in that in the first the main issue seems to be the avoidance of suffering or distress, whereas in the second the main issue seems to be the information for a proper choice.

Before considering these three categories in more detail, we would like to dispose of one attempt medical workers in particular sometimes make to avoid the responsibility of deciding whether or not to tell the truth: the appeal to human fallibility and scientific uncertainty. For example, when asked why he did not tell someone that he was dying, a doctor may reply 'But I don't *know* that he is – I may have got the diagnosis wrong – miracles do happen', etc. Now it may be a case where the doctor thinks there really *is* room for doubt; obviously in such a case he is *not* presenting the truth if he presents as a certainty what is only a possibility. (He may well still have an obligation to mention the possibility.) It may also be true that medicine is so complex that certainty is *never* possible, and that even where everyone concerned *feels* certain, their feelings are not justified. But even if this is so, it does not prevent a doctor from saying 'To the best of our knowledge ... ' or 'We're pretty sure that ... '. He must remember, however, that what is important is what is actually *conveyed*, and guard against suggesting that he thinks there is still hope when he does not. It might perhaps be added that this *general* scepticism about the status of medical knowledge seems much less in evidence in other contexts!

Let us now turn to the first of our three categories, taking as our main example the situation where a patient is dying. One of the reasons advanced for concealing the gravity of his position from a patient, and sometimes from his relatives as well, is the wish to save him (and them) unnecessary *distress*. Two questions arise about this concern: first, are the *facts* correct, (*does* such a policy lessen distress?); and second, what is the *force* of the consideration (even if we grant that it does, is this sufficient reason for withholding the truth?)

On the factual question it is impossible to say anything conclusive, especially as every case must differ in this respect. But there is certainly evidence that in many cases distress is *increased* by a policy of concealment. For example, the patient may sense that his state is worse than anyone admits, but cannot discuss his fears with anyone and so is left to face the prospect of death alone; or he feels cut off from his family (when they know the truth and he does not) but he does not understand the sense of strain which comes between them. Again, where relatives are not given the true state of affairs, death will come as a shock as well as a sadness and this increases its distressfulness. Moreover, a refusal to allow the patient to realize that he is dying cuts him off from the positive help nowadays available for just such patients in the form of the hospice movement, or discussions with social workers specially trained for working in this sensitive area.

Even if it were established that in general, or in a particular case, distress could be *saved* by withholding the truth, this does not settle the issue; for there are other countervailing considerations in favour of telling the truth. First of all, the patient's *choices* are highly relevant here. If what we said earlier about liberty is correct, we should respect a person's *desire* to know the truth. Now there can clearly be a *conflict* here between saving a person distress and acceding to his wishes: a doctor can be fairly sure that his patient who is now so keen to know all will not like what he hears. But we think that it would be patronizing and lacking in respect for liberty for a doctor to decide on his patient's behalf that comfort is more important than knowledge when the patient wishes knowledge. After all, there is nothing odd in preferring truth to comfort.

If priority is to be given to patients' choice where it conflicts with the minimizing of distress, it follows that a person who asks not to be told the truth should *not* be told it, even if we think he will be happier knowing it. This of course leaves in the middle those who neither ask to know nor ask not to know. Some construe a patient's silence as a tacit refusal to be told, some as a longing to know coupled with fear. Something turns on how far genuine opportunity has been given for him to ask. If he *has* been given this and does *not* ask, then judgment of what to do is problematic, and must depend partly on guesses as to his present wishes, partly on guesses as to the likely result of telling him and partly on weighing up the points which follow.

The second consideration which tells against concealing the truth is the *general* results of a practice of doing so. Since it is generally known that doctors often give a more optimistic picture than is really warranted, there is widespread lack of confidence in their more vague or optimistic pronouncements. (One of the authors, who is from a medical family, has several times been asked whether doctors 'really mean cancer' by various phrases.) The result of this lack of confidence is not only that well-meant deception is often unsuccessful, but also that genuine good tidings are not believed. These considerations weigh to some extent in favour of truthfulness, even in cases where a situation taken in isolation might favour deception.

The third consideration is that it can plausibly be said that people have a right to know the truth about themselves. In saying this, we are not merely repeating in other words what has already been said about respecting a person's desire to know the truth. That point could indeed be put in the language of rights, in terms of a person's general right, other things being equal, not to be thwarted in the pursuit of his ends. But what we have in mind here is a special right, concerning truth as a special benefit.

On what is this special right based? We might at first think of it as resting on the trust the patient has in the doctor. But the patient does not always trust the doctor, so a universal right to truth cannot be founded on trust. Nor is it clear that such trust, where it exists, must be seen as including trusting the doctor to tell the *truth*. Certainly the patient trusts the doctor to look after his welfare, but whether that welfare includes knowing the truth is exactly what is in question. Of course in the case of private medicine one might hold that there is a contractual *undertaking*, explicit or implicit, to hand over the expert knowledge the patient has paid for. But this idea cannot account for a general obligation to tell the truth. Now part of the importance of truth is that it is needed to inform *decisions*. If self-determination is indeed important, then it is also important to give the chooser the tools for its proper exercise. It might be thought that making informed decisions is relevant only in our *second* category of cases, where the safety of possible treatment is in question. But this is not the case. If a man knows he has not long to live, he will probably adopt a different plan of life from that he would adopt if he thought he had many years in front of him. For one thing he will have affairs both secular and spiritual to settle before he dies. (It is in this context that discussions between medical workers and social workers, and social workers and patients, may be helpful.

For the social worker has within his professional competence the knowledge which will enable a dying patient to reach informed decisions about the future provision for his family, the disposal of his goods, etc.) Truth about his own life and death is thus not just something a man may want, but also a part of the framework within which he decides what else to pursue. That is why we have spoken about a *right* to know the truth.

It may be retorted here that since *no one* knows when he is going to die (a fatal accident can befall anyone at any time) there cannot be a *right* to such knowledge. Now it is true that there cannot be such a right absolutely in the abstract and in general. But what we are discussing here is whether a person has the right to be given by others knowledge of this very important kind which the others happen to possess. To withhold knowledge on *this* ground would be like withholding a medicine on the ground that it did not work on everyone.

Before leaving the discussion of our first category of cases perhaps we may mention a special type of case: that where knowledge of the patient's condition will undoubtedly make him worse. (We say 'undoubtedly' because there is presumably some risk of this in other cases.) Here the question is not so much whether the doctor *should* tell the patient the truth as whether he logically *can* tell him, since the act of telling will *ex hypothesi* alter the situation. (One might compare here the dilemma of a Chancellor of the Exchequer who thinks that he may have to devalue the pound: he cannot say that this is a possibility without making it inevitable.) It looks as though the doctor may need to err on the optimistic side in such a way that what is over-favourable if regarded as a description has some chance of *coming* true as a prediction.

Let us now turn to the second kind of case which raises problems for truthfulness: the possible dangers of proposed treatments or procedures. The medical profession in general pays homage to the notion of '*informed* consent', and certainly to expect patients to consent to treatment without understanding its implications, or to choose between alternatives of which they do not understand the true nature, is to fail to respect their capacity for self-determination. But sometimes in the Press and elsewhere doctors are quoted as saying things like 'I don't bother patients with accounts of possible side-effects and hazards – it's far too complicated and worrying for them – it's the doctor's responsibility to make his own mind up.'

Let us take each of these points in turn, beginning with the complications. No doubt some issues are too complex for some patients. But it sometimes seems as though doctors are confusing the *factors*, which are normally complex, with the *issues*, which can be very simple. For example, the issue might be a choice between a very safe contraceptive with slight risk of various side-effects, many of which can be specified, and a less reliable contraceptive with no dangers but considerable inconvenience. The factors here, by which we mean such things as the ways in which hormones work and the manner in which they can affect blood pressure, might well be rather too complex for the lay mind; but then a patient does not need to understand *these* to make a reasonable decision. Again, it sometimes seems as though doctors assume patients do not understand the issues simply because they choose differently from the doctor. Thus, doctors were heard to say 'All these mothers who won't have their children immunized against whooping cough don't understand how *remote* the dangers of brain damage are, in comparison with the danger of death from whooping cough.' But it is certainly *intelligible* to prefer a greater risk of death to a smaller risk of what is surely 'a fate worse than death' and moreover one inflicted on the child as a result of one's own decision. Similarly it is intelligible (even if wrong?) for the mother to ignore those considerations about the community as a whole which will rightly interest the doctor.

The point about distressing the patient recalls our earlier discussion about comfort versus truth. It seems to us patronizing for the doctor to try to save the patient worry and distress at the cost of preventing him from making genuine decisions about his future. Responsible adult life is full of situations where people have to choose between alternatives, both painful, and in no other sphere would it be thought proper for someone else to decide.

The claim that 'it's the doctor's responsibility to make up his own mind' can sound like an accusation that those who leave too much decision in the hands of the patients are evading a responsibility which is properly theirs. But this is not really the case, as no one except the patient himself can decide basic priorities, such as whether a painful and restricted life is preferable to a risky operation which if successful will restore full powers. And there is no right answer here. Of course patients may say 'You decide, doctor' or 'What would *you* do?' and in such cases the doctor has been given a mandate by the patients. He might think it correct to *invite* such a mandate, by saying 'We've got a problem here – there are various possibilities but they all have some drawbacks – shall I tell you about them, or shall I just decide in the best way I can?' But such doctors should remain aware that they are making decisions in the light of priorities and schemes of values which may be different from those of the patient. In this context discussions between doctors and social workers and social workers and patients may be helpful, just for the reason that the social worker may have a different order of priorities from the doctor and therefore see things differently. Co-operation between doctor and social workers may be good for the patient even if, or especially because, they have different values.

Let us now turn briefly to the third kind of case in which truth is a problem – the case of drug trials. The problem here is acute, in that in some contexts an essential feature of a valid trial is that the patients should *not* know in detail what is going on: the so-called blind trials. The ethics of drug trials have been discussed in detail by others.[9] The general principles which we have outlined, however, give some guidance: the patient has a right to the truth which is not absolute (it can be over-ridden if sufficient benefit can be gained thereby) but cannot be ignored. This principle would suggest that the patient has at least the right to as much information as is consistent with a valid trial. For example, while he often cannot in the nature of the case be told whether he is being given a new drug or an old one, he can be told that a trial of a new drug is proposed, asked if he will take part and told whether he can hope for personal benefit or is being invited to contribute altruistically.

In this discussion about respect for truth we have not tried to say that it is *always* right to tell the truth. There is no reason why this should be thought true in medicine and social work when it is not (by most people) thought true in life in general. But our aim has been to suggest that truth has a claim of its own which can sometimes be ignored. Of course nothing we have said absolves the doctor or social worker from the obligation to tell the truth in the most compassionate way he can. In other words, our claim that telling the truth may be justified, even when it causes suffering, does not entail that the caring worker is entitled to cause further unnecessary suffering by the way he tells it.

It should be noted that in this section we have been concerned with the nature of the caring worker's duty to provide relevant *information* about his patient's condition or situation. Does the caring worker have a duty to convey his moral *judgment on* or other *valuation of* the patient's or client's situation? This is a question which arises more for the social worker than the medical worker, and we shall discuss it separately (see pp. 87-90).

3 The politics
of the
caring professions

The free market state

The caring professions make the largest contribution to what in Britain are called the social services. To have a proper grasp of the background to the existence of the social services we need to take a step back and consider the reasons for the existence of the State itself. What is a state for? How can the existence of a system of government, a legal and political organization, be justified? The various answers to this question make up the history of political thought from the seventeenth century to the twentieth.

Our strategy in this chapter will be to begin with an outline of the theory of the *laissez-faire* free market state as it was expressed in the eighteenth century by its greatest exponent, Adam Smith, and then to go on to consider moral defects in the *laissez-faire* system which are thought to be repaired by the social services of the present-day Welfare State. We shall draw attention to five main defects, or types of defect, in the *laissez-faire* system: its failure to accommodate the idea that a government has a moral duty to further the health and welfare, not just of the community as a whole, but of each individual within it; the encouragement it gives by means of its economic competitiveness to the creation of social inequality; its consumer, non-idealistic conception of human beings; its commercialization of caring relationships; and its failure to encourage the sense of a community and the growth of a spirit of fellowship within it. In each case we shall consider how far the defects can be remedied by a welfare-state system. We shall then discuss in more detail the question of state provision of health care, considering various gradations between a purely *laissez-faire* and a purely socialist solution to the problem. For reasons which will emerge, we shall not always be optimistic about the success of these alternatives or how far in the end they represent a significant moral advance on a *laissez-faire* system. We shall finally consider the criteria for fixing the wages of health workers, as a further illustration of that interaction of the principles of equity, freedom and the common good which forms the basis of political discussion.

The political philosophy of *laissez-faire*, indeed most political philosophy, begins from the obvious truth that human beings are individually not self-sufficient and have therefore been obliged for their mutual succour to do what their differing aptitudes would have encouraged them to do in any case – create division of labour. But a market is required for the ordering and distribution of the goods which human needs require. Markets are therefore necessary for the continued existence of society. But markets cannot exist outside a framework of law, since law is required both to provide an authoritative definition of economic contracts and to afford protection against the subtly unscrupulous and the crudely criminal. People therefore have every incentive to give up some of their natural rights in return for the greater degree of protection and organization supplied by some central system of government and law.

This is a brief account of what came to be known as the *laissez-faire* view of the State. Such a view presupposes the existence of a free market economy and ascribes to a government the largely negative functions of protecting people and their property from enemies outside and inside the State, and enforcing legal contracts. Of course, even in terms of relatively pure versions of *laissez-faire* philosophy it is difficult to confine government action to negative functions. Adam Smith, for example, a high priest of this view of the State, realized that a government would need to intervene in economic affairs to prevent the setting-up of monopolies, or to carry out expensive public works, such as bridge building, the cost of which could not be carried by individuals or small corporations, or to regulate conditions for apprenticeships.[1]

Such governmental interventions in economic affairs are clearly consistent with a *laissez-faire* view of the State, but can a *laissez-faire* political philosophy consistently advocate policies which can in any sense be called 'welfare' policies? Adam Smith certainly thought that he could assign to the government responsibility for mitigating the brutalizing effects on workers of the division of labour. This is an aspect of the well-known problem, made familiar to us by Marxists, of the 'alienation' of the worker. Now there is no reason why the division of labour, properly so-called, should brutalize anyone, and not all thinkers have held that it did. For example, Plato sees the State as founded on the division of labour, but for him division of labour springs from a prior diversity of individual endowment, so that the individual can find the fulfilment of his nature in the craftsmanship of his labour.[2] The *Wealth of Nations* differs from the *Republic*, however, in two vital respects. In the first place, for Adam Smith division of labour is not *founded* on diversity of endowment, but rather causally determines diversity of occupation. In other words, no self-fulfilment can (logically) be found in the division of labour because, according to Smith, the self has no nature to be fulfilled until one is created by the division of labour. In the second place, although Adam Smith speaks of the division of labour, he is in fact mainly concerned with the *subdivision* of labour, and it is this which is objectionable, if anything is, in man's economic life. In other words, while someone may find some self-fulfilment if he earns his living as an electrician or a truck driver, he will not find self-fulfilment from his work at the side of a conveyor belt.

Now, if we take into account that Adam Smith was writing just before the Industrial Revolution, he can be said to show for his period remarkably realistic, indeed pessimistic, awareness of the effects of industrialization. Thus, speaking of a workman he says,

His dexterity at his own particular trade seems to be acquired at the expense of his intellectual social and martial virtues. But in every improved and civilised society this is the state into which the labouring poor, that is, the great body of the people, must necessarily fall, unless government takes some pains to prevent it.[3]

And further on he speaks of a workman as suffering a 'sort of mental mutilation, deformity and wretchedness'. Hence, Adam Smith does show some awareness of the human costs of economic growth. Moreover, he points towards at least a partial remedy: a government must take 'some pains' to prevent this intellectual deformity, and what it must do is to provide a system of education and

> impose upon almost the whole body of the people the necessity of acquiring those most essential parts of education by obliging every man to undergo an examination or probation in them before he can obtain the freedom in a corporation or be allowed to set up any trade.[4]

By compulsory education, then, Adam Smith hoped to protect the individual against the intellectual and social ravages of the division of labour and to foster his freedom. There is then in Adam Smith an awareness of a minimal welfare function for the State which, in a Scottish Presbyterian way, he sees in terms of the need for education and examinations.

In addition to this minimal *welfare* function a *laissez-faire* political philosophy could consistently advocate certain services vital to *health care* – it could insist on high standards of public health such as come from clean drains, unpolluted air and so on. The argument is that even on a negative conception of government there would be a requirement to protect citizens from disease, and no clear line can be drawn between this and the positive furthering of the health of the inhabitants by public health legislation. It is important to stress this because it is fashionable to despise *laissez-faire* political philosophy on the grounds, among others, that it has nothing positive to advocate on health care. Yet if it can consistently advocate public health legislation it can achieve as much improvement in the nation's health as a national health service, for an adequate system of sanitation and other public health measures have probably done more for the health of the nation than any hospitals.

Nevertheless, despite this defence of *laissez-faire* political philosophy, it could be said that we have not touched on the central moral defects of a free market economy and the *laissez-faire* system of government that goes with it. The most common defect of such a system is said to be that it is based on self-interest, and a society based on self-interest will exhibit at least some of the undesirable characteristics of a Hobbesian 'state of nature'. The self-interested character of a market economy has its classic description in the following passage from Adam Smith's *Wealth of Nations*:

> In almost every other race of animals, each individual, when it is grown up to maturity, is entirely independent, and in the natural state has occasion for the assistance of no other living creature. But man has almost constant occasion for the help of his brethren, and it is not for him to expect it from their benevolence only. He is more likely to prevail if he can interest their self-love in his favour, and show them that it is for their own advantage to do for him what he requires of them...It is not from the benevolence of the butcher, the brewer, or the baker that we expect our dinner, but from their regard to their own self-interest. We address ourselves, not to their humanity, but to their self-love, and never talk to them of our own necessities, but of their advantages.[5]

It is not strictly accurate, however, to describe the economic relation as one of self-interest, or egoism. It is certainly true that each party in an economic exchange is attempting to maximize gain for himself, not for the other party. But by 'gain' we mean here a realization of what the agents severally consider good, and this need not be egoistic at all, far less selfish. Thus a person's conception of what is good may include the realization of the good of others. More helpful than the term 'self-interest' is the one introduced last century by the Rev. Philip Wicksteed, 'non-tuism'[6]:

> What makes an economic transaction is that I am not considering you except as a link in the chain, or considering your desires except as the means by which I may gratify those of someone else – not necessarily myself. The economic relation does not exclude from my mind everyone but me; it potentially includes everyone but you.

Or again:

> ...the note of a business transaction between A and B is not that A's ego is consciously in his mind, but that, however many

the *alteri* are, B is not one of them; and B, in like manner, whether he is thinking only of his own *ego* or of innumerable *alteri*, is not thinking of A.

Thus he concludes that: 'The specific characteristic of an economic relation is not its "egoism" but its "non-tuism."

A relation of this 'non-tuistic' sort is not simply regulative of conduct in the market – it is not just a guiding principle – but it is a necessary constitutive condition of a market in the sense that where it does not obtain we do not have a market, but some other relationship between people. Whatever the defects of the market mechanism, therefore, it is superficial to attack it on the grounds that it is essentially based on self-interest.

Moreover, as we have seen, there is a positive safeguard against the supposed corruption caused by the desire for profit to be found in the market: an economic relation is also by its very nature a *juridical* relation. There are two reasons for saying this. The first is that an economic order assumes that there is an already existing system of rights, in that exchange is always at a 'price', and 'price' is an agreed exchange ratio. The second is that the establishment of an economic relation is *ipso facto* the establishment of a juridical relation in so far as it constitutes a 'contract' defining the rights and duties of the parties. In other words, a *purely* economic relation is an abstraction; all economic relations are integrated with juridical relations and the self-seeking of the parties is thereby limited. Hobbes' man ruthlessly pursuing his self-interest is not in an economic order until the sovereign establishes a legal order. If we were attempting to seek a complete definition of an economic order we should of course need to refer to at least two other factors – the influence of scarcity, and of political conditions which allow a measure of freedom of choice – but for the purposes of this discussion the important point is that the 'non-tuism' of the economic relation is regulated by being from the outset a juridical relation.[7]

The relief of needs

We have seen that it is superficial to stigmatize the market state as being essentially selfish or egoistic. But such a state, at least in its pure form, does have various deficiencies. First of all it might be said that on this model of the State the government would quite simply be abrogating its responsibilities towards the needy. Certainly, Adam Smith would not have seen it as part of the function of the State to provide the extensive health and social services which go to make up the British Welfare State. On Adam Smith's *laissez-faire* system medical care and what we now call social services would be left entirely to private enterprise: those who can afford it pay for their medical treatment or other services on a business footing, either directly or through insurance schemes, while government interferes only to the extent that it interferes in other commercial enterprises: that is to say, it enforces contracts, hears suits for damage and tries to prevent fraud, perhaps in this case by insisting on qualifications for medical practitioners and other health and welfare workers.

There is, of course, nothing in the concept of a free market economy which is inimical to the growth of *charitable* institutions – indeed, as a matter of historical fact, charitable institutions seem to flourish better in a free market economy than in other economic systems. Nevertheless, the provisions of charitable institutions afford too haphazard a basis for such important services as health and welfare. In any case, it might be said that health care and the relief of other basic needs are basic human rights; if this is so, receiving them should not have to depend on people's goodwill, however forthcoming that goodwill is. Of course replacing a *laissez-faire* system with some other system might mean a loss of that worthwhile thing, exercise of the motive of charity. But there are some things which are so important that getting them done properly is more important than getting them done inadequately from the right motive. In any case, scope would remain in any scheme for the exercise of charity. We have today, for example, charities which support medical research, and which may feel justified in pursuing projects with a high risk of failure which those bodies using tax-payers' extorted money feel unjustified in supporting.

The inadequacy of the *laissez-faire* system in this respect does not mean that there are no difficulties with the notion of state provision of health and welfare services. Criticisms of such state provision are of two main kinds. The first kind, which we may call intrinsic criticism, maintains that the needs which the State purports to meet are *not* in fact more adequately met in a state system. The second kind maintains that even if needs *are* more adequately met in such a system, the price for this result is too high: in other words, too many other values have to be sacrificed.

Intrinsic criticisms of state provision for the needy can take various forms. The first form is of the 'killing the goose which laid the golden eggs' type. State welfare services are very expensive and have to be paid for by very heavy taxes, but such taxes discourage enterprise and spending, and so make the country poorer by depressing industry: there will therefore be less and less to spend on the social services and at the same time more of the poverty and unemployment which fosters the need for them. This 'golden eggs' line of criticism of the Welfare State is of course very familiar. It should be noted, however, that it rests on a question of *degree*: that is, it maintains that there is a point beyond which state provision of welfare services is counter-productive. It does nothing to show that any modification of the pure *laissez-faire* state is always counter-productive. From this point of view, then, some kind of mixed system will be the most satisfactory: one which achieves the optimum balance between the creation of wealth and state provision of needs.

Another familiar line of intrinsic criticism is that state provision of welfare is necessarily inefficient and clumsy. An operation on such a scale, it is argued, is bound to involve a lot of waste and to fail to relieve the real cases of extreme need in its efforts to provide blanket coverage for all. This is again a criticism which rests on a question of degree. It may well be that an extremely comprehensive system incurs difficulties of this kind which a mixed system could avoid; but those in favour of extensive state welfare provision will point out that a partial system has the problem of drawing lines between extreme need and moderate need – a process sometimes so invidious that it too may be counter-productive.

The extrinsic criticisms of the Welfare State's system of providing relief from need are again very familiar: that such a system stifles liberty, and that it exalts material provision at the expense of other good things and qualities. We have already mentioned one example of the latter point when we said that there may be less exercise of private charity on a state welfare scheme; it is often said also that such schemes sap character by removing responsibility for one's own welfare. Once again, these criticisms turn on questions of degree. In the political situation, there is always a necessity to balance liberty against equality and both against other values, and the real question always is: what *degree* of one may be sacrificed to gain what degree of another? Different types of political solution to this question emphasize different values. Later in this chapter we shall try to show how the competing values bear on two questions: the provision of health care, and the assessment of salaries for caring workers.

Equality and ideals

A second major criticism of a *laissez-faire* market state is that such a state must be *competitive*, and in so far as it is competitive it will produce unequal satisfaction. Markets are competitive in a double sense: consumers compete with producers or retailers for the maximization of their personal gain, and producers or retailers compete with each other for possession of the market. Competition of this sort, even if regulated by a juridical order, will result in considerable inequalities, in that some members of society will be much more successful than others, and this success will be passed on to their children. A market mechanism therefore makes for social inequality in the distribution of consumer goods.

The failure to accommodate the claims of equality is a feature, not merely of the particular political system we are considering, but also of the broadly utilitarian moral stance which underlies it. For one great danger of a utilitarian approach, as Mill the great utilitarian himself realized, albeit imperfectly, is that it seems to say nothing about the *distribution* of good. It would be perfectly in keeping with utilitarianism to pursue policies as a result of which the majority are better off but some people decidedly not so. In the medical and social services this kind of policy decision tends to arise in terms of the allocation of resources. Suppose a medical or social worker is faced with a potential client who will be extremely expensive in his use of resources: for example, a patient who needs renal dialysis or a depressive near-alcoholic who needs hours of social work time. In terms of *maximizing* benefit to the community at large, it might well be better to ignore altogether the needs of such people and spend the resources of time and money on those whose plight is less serious.

But this policy seems wrong to most people in that it ignores the right of each individual to *equal consideration*. No one may be regarded simply as expendable for the sake of the good of others.

This notion of 'equal consideration', however, needs considerably more examination, and we shall look at it further before returning to the *laissez-faire* state. In some philosophical contexts the demand for equal consideration is merely a demand for *consistent* treatment as between one person and another: in other words, a demand that people be treated in accordance with some *rule* which can be formulated. This demand for consistency seems to clash with the more personalized aspects of casework which stress the impossibility of general rules and the uniqueness of the individual situation. But where benefits are being distributed, clients and patients are keen to demand consistency ('why won't you give to me what you gave to him?') and regard as unfair any difference of this kind which seems to be an arbitrary exception. Consistency, then, is necessary if distribution of benefit (and of course medical treatment and social work service are themselves benefits) is to be seen as fair. But it is not *sufficient* for fairness. As we have seen, a principle of distribution which could be applied quite consistently, such as 'never spend time on an alcoholic', might itself be unfair. To get nearer to the *moral* principle of equal consideration, we need to find some way of ruling out such possibilities.

It is tempting to try to do this by saying that what is required is not consistency but an actual *equality* of treatment. But this is not satisfactory either, as some people need much more help than others and no one thinks it reasonable to spend the same amount of time and money whatever the problem. What is required is that all differences of treatment be based on a criterion which will group like cases together, and distinguish unlike cases, for *morally appropriate* reasons. In this context the obvious criterion is *need*, since the aim of proffering help is to meet needs: those whose need is greatest should get more help than those whose need is less, and those whose need is equal should get equal help. This principle of justified differences in treatment based on the criterion of differing degrees of need is neatly illustrated by those benefits which are scaled according to the size of the family which is to receive them.

We can call this requirement that any differences of treatment be based on morally appropriate reasons a principle of *equity*. Equity is not the same as equality, since it says not only that like cases must be treated equally but also that unlike cases must be treated unequally. As we have seen, equity presupposes a *criterion* for justifiable differences in the way people are treated. In the context of the social services this will normally be need, but others are sometimes relevant. For example, it is often thought that punishments should be distributed according to *desert*: in other words, those whose degree of guilt is the same should get the same punishment. Social workers sometimes have to cope with the resentment of those who feel they have been punished more severely than someone who was equally guilty. Again, some educational benefits are supposed to be distributed according to *capacity* to benefit from them, and competitive jobs according to *merit*: social workers dealing with, say, coloured youths have to cope with inequity in these spheres. We shall consider more criteria relevant to equity when we discuss a just wage later in the chapter.

So far the kind of equality in decision-making which we have described is both derivative and relative: *derivative*, in that it depends on another value, such as need or merit, before it comes into operation; and *relative*, in that it involves equality only with others in the same group, not with everyone. There is, however, a type of equality which we may call egalitarian equality, which seems to be neither derivative nor relative; it advocates that all people be treated equally for equality's sake, not just in the course of pursuing other values. A principle of egalitarian equality entails, not only trying when serving people's needs to do so in an equitable manner, but also redistributing benefits simply to make people more equal when need is not in question. In practice, of course, this distinction between equity and egalitarianism is not clear-cut. What one group sees as organizing taxation and benefits in an equitable way proportionate to the *needs* of all concerned, another group sees as 'the egalitarian politics of envy'. Again, what can be construed in a given society as *needed* depends in part on an egalitarian consideration, viz., what other people have: in a society where most people have television, a mains water supply is not a luxury but a need. The spirit of egalitarian equality is very important for our present purposes, since it lies behind much welfare legislation and motivates many social workers.

We spoke just now of the egalitarians' aim to 'make people more equal'. But the question immediately arises – equal in what respect? For it is possible to draw a broad contrast between the ideal of equality of *opportunity* – equality in the starting and running conditions of the race of life – and equality of *satisfaction* – the ideal of proceeding side by side throughout the race to a 'tie' at the finish. It is fairly common for those of moderate opinion to commit themselves to the first of these ideals rather than the second. But it seems clear that the second also is aimed at by many politicians at the present time. Moreover, the truth may be (although believers in equality of opportunity have not always faced up to it) that the first cannot be secured in independence of the second. For if you provide equality of opportunity, then, granted the truth of some uncontroversial propositions about the variation in human ability, industry, etc., the tendency will be towards inequality of achievement and reward; and you then cannot prevent the more successful from using their resources to procure advantageous opportunities for their own children or friends without destroying to a greater or lesser extent the *value* of the reward of their own success. Perhaps, then, we must say that if the welfare services are really concerned with equality as an ideal they are concerned to secure in the last resort not just 'equal opportunities' but 'equal satisfactions'.

So far, then, we have considered two applications of the moral idea of equality: the relative equality, or equity, which derives from the application of some moral criterion of distribution such as need or desert, and egalitarian equality which seems to be neither relative nor derivative. Both these notions of equality, however, presuppose some more fundamental kind of equality in terms of which it is assumed that all human beings ought to be regarded as equal. Egalitarian equality assumes that *all* human beings ought to have equal satisfactions, and does not exclude any group from its scope. Equity, although it does not say that everyone should be treated equally, incorporates the demand that differences in treatment must be *morally justified*: in other words, the presumption is that people should be treated equally *unless* there is moral warrant for treating them differently. Both principles therefore rule out the option of leaving some group out of one's moral calculations altogether. Thus respect for equity precludes us from saying 'Don't bother about the alcoholics' or 'Don't bother about the mentally deficient'.

But if the underlying equality is supposed to involve the notion that there is a respect in which people *are* equal as a matter of fact, it is clearly mistaken. People are manifestly *unequal* in physique, in mental capacity, in physical attractiveness, in moral goodness, in any respect that can be thought of. We do however speak of people as of equal *worth* or *value*. Given that people are *not* in fact equal, can any sense be made of this idea?

The notion of human beings as of equal worth does make sense if it is regarded not as a statement of fact about human beings but as a principle prescribing how they are to be treated. The importance of the principle does not lie in its stress on *equality*, but in its stress on human worth. The point is that each individual human being is to be treated as having worth or value in himself. He does not have a price – he is not replaceable by anything else, even by another human being – he has what Kant calls *dignity*, the value of something which is irreplaceable.[8] This is again the principle of respect for the individual, and it carries with it the idea that no one's claims may be ignored, however great the gain to others, because a price cannot be put on any individual's welfare. This point can be put in terms of equality by saying that everyone is of equal importance, but the equality is after all *derivative*, in the sense we distinguished earlier; it depends on another moral value, that of respect for the individual. We can depict both equity and egalitarian equality as manifestations of respect for the individual, deployed in a social context; both, but particularly egalitarian equality, are also called social justice.

The welfare services are committed to social justice in so far as it is pre-eminently in the name of social justice and for the sake of increasing social equality that a great deal of welfare legislation has been introduced. But the question remains: how important, after all, is social justice? In discussing this question there is always a tendency to rate social justice too highly: indeed it has a privileged position in the rhetoric of the welfare services. Yet there are two grounds on which it is reasonable to have reservations about exclusive concentration on social justice as a value. Neither of these has any tendency to suggest that social justice is anything but a worthwhile value, but both in different ways suggest that it can be a mistake to concentrate too much on social justice.

The first of these we will mention but not discuss because it raises questions of political economy which are not our present concern. It is a criticism of the type we called 'golden eggs': namely, that legislation designed to interfere with the operation of the market mechanism, whether in the name of social justice or not, will do just that, and one result is likely to be that that mechanism will not work so well. The first to suffer from this are frequently those very people for whom welfare legislation is intended. The development of this point raises not unfamiliar economic and political controversies, but it does not become irrelevant for all that.

Let us rather concentrate on a second ground for having reservations about an exclusive commitment to social justice as a value. This ground concerns the distinction between a person's interests or satisfactions and what we earlier called his improvement: other qualities essential to his self, such as his abilities to be autonomous, self-determining and to have a sense of responsibility, and his intellectual, cultural and personal development. Social justice comes into the picture only in connection with the former, but if we fail to distinguish the two we shall come to think that the former is all that matters in all our dealings with other persons. There are practical dangers for welfare thinking in this confusion. Thus it follows from the earlier argument that where social justice is concerned, equality of satisfaction is the ideal. It is therefore easy to think, as many social reformers perhaps do think, that the whole purpose of social living is to secure as equal a distribution of as much happiness as can be brought about, without regard to *quality* of life. And the problem is not merely that the pursuit of social justice *ignores* the quality of life; in some ways it may be inimical to it. Thus, for example, it is maintained by some that too much reliance on welfare benefits can sap initiative and sense of responsibility; or that attempts to make education more egalitarian have resulted in a net loss in quality; or that governmental spending on social services has impoverished the arts both by removing subsidies from them and by overtaxing the middle classes who are their chief supporters.

Somehow or other, then, we must strike a balance between the claims of other ideals and those of social justice. There are no rules for doing so, but a minimum principle would be that where what is vaguely referred to as the 'standard of living' of a section of the community falls below a certain level then 'social justice' becomes a priority for that section. One way of developing the idea of a minimum principle of social equality might be to distinguish between a person's basic needs and his more complex wants. The fulfilment of his basic needs – food, shelter, medical care and so on – can then be regarded as constituting legitimate social rights about which there can be no moral reservations. Indeed, the fulfilment of these minimum social rights can be regarded as a necessary condition for the exercise of any rights whatsoever: there can be no rights to life or liberty without bread to sustain the possessors of these rights. But problems arise when we begin to extend the range of these social rights, and those problems are acute because a person's pursuit of his own satisfactions can come to dominate all aspects of his social life. His consumption increases and his fellow-citizens claim that they have a right to equal consumption. This is the pathology of advanced industrial societies. There is therefore a problem as to the relative weight to be given to social justice in this sense as opposed to other values; too much emphasis on it may encourage the consumer conception of the self already implicit in the operation of the market.

This remark brings us to the third criticism levelled at the *laissez-faire* market society: critics of markets, from Plato on, have pointed out that there is an inevitable transition from the attempt to satisfy basic needs to the attempt to satisfy wants quite unconnected with needs. In other words, a market gradually but inevitably generates inordinate desires for its goods, and this is morally corrupting because eventually no one has a conception of himself other than in hedonistic terms, as a consumer. There is a good deal of force in this criticism, and indeed Adam Smith was himself fully aware of the strength of it, referring to commodities as 'trifles of frivolous utility'.

As we have seen, however, defenders of the market have retorted that the self presupposed in welfare legislation is in fact the very same consumer self, and that the criticism that the free market economy trivializes human life by encouraging a consumer conception of the self and its interests can be turned also on the supporters of welfare legislation: that in the name of social justice they remove from a person his responsibility for his own and his family's health, future security, old age and so on, and thereby remove from the scope of his own will those matters which ought to be of deepest concern to him. In other words, defenders of the market maintain that if the ideal of social justice is realized a person's *area for choice* will be restricted to the trivialities or luxuries of life, and as a result his conception of himself will again be in terms of his interests as a consumer.

These criticisms, whether levelled at the *laissez-faire* market economy or at a welfare state, need careful examination. As stated above, both criticisms contrast a concern with basic needs, which is commended, with a concern with 'luxuries' which is regarded as trivial. But if the suggestion is that everything which is not a basic need is trivial, it is clearly mistaken: on the contrary, it might be argued that basic needs constitute merely the *means* of life and what is really important is what kind of life is lived through these means. We come nearer to the heart of these criticisms if we see them as directed against *material consumption*. But what from one point of view is material consumption can from another point of view be an attempt to create something beautiful which reflects individual choice and taste – an artistic activity. What we must say, then, is that any system which encourages consumption *as such* is deficient, and needs to be supplemented by concern for other ideals: ideals of character and personality, ideals of beauty and knowledge. These are wanted for their own sake by many people and their attainment contributes to their happiness; but they are regarded as ideal values which are important not just because they are wanted.

We might sum up this discussion of the market, equality and ideals by saying that if the market is allowed to operate without interference we have a *legalized* barbarism, for buying and selling will be the main activity and profit and loss the main value. But if social justice is pursued as the only additional ideal we shall finish up with what may be called a *moralized* barbarism. It will be 'moralized' because it will display a concern for others which is excellent in itself, but it will be 'barbarism' because it will *not* be much concerned with values other than self-satisfaction. What is necessary for a morally healthy society, one with the energy to develop itself and to flourish, is that its members should recognize that there are two quite different ways in which we may exhibit respect for our fellows. There is, on the one hand, respect

for their *social rights*; and here we should be thoroughly egalitarian. But so long as we limit ourselves to this aspect of the matter
we are acting as though happiness were the only good. There is
also, however, the respect we show to our fellows in treating
them as co-operators in the service of *ideals*, some of which may
indeed be community ideals. For example, these might include
stress on 'quality of architecture' as distinct from 'quantity of
housing', or on the preservation of the natural environment as
distinct from, or even as opposed to, energy-intensive modes of
production. Ideals of this sort have nothing to do with rights,
justice, equality or inequality, and are only contingently connected with welfare goods, but they are nevertheless essential to
the culture and the dignity of a society.

The caring relationship

A fourth line of criticism made of the market state is that within it
relationships between caring workers and their clients or patients
become merely business transactions whereas, it is said, they
should be personal relationships. This criticism needs extended
discussion. We shall consider first what a relationship is and then
go on to discuss what kinds of relationship are possible or
desirable in a caring situation and what happens to these in a
market state.

We can use the word 'relationship' in two ways: to stand for the
situation, bond or occasion which links two or more people, or to
stand for the attitudes which people so linked have to each other.[9]
As examples of the first kind of relationship we might mention
kinship, marriage, business association, meeting through contin-
gencies or emergencies, etc. As examples of the second kind we
might mention fear, pride, respect, envy, contempt, etc. Thus
someone seeing an adult with a child might ask 'What is the
relationship between that pair?', and receive an answer in terms
of the first kind of relationship: 'teacher and pupil', 'father and
son', etc. Or he might ask 'What sort of relationship do Jones and
his son have?', and receive an answer in terms of the second kind
of relationship: 'Jones has a great affection for his son but his son
has nothing but contempt for him.'

The two kinds of relationship are connected in various complex
ways. For example, if the situation is a business transaction then

the attitude of the parties would not characteristically be one of, say, affection, although there is no logical impediment to such an attitude developing out of the business transactions. Again, if people in one situation develop certain attitudes towards each other then new situations may develop out of the attitudes, and marriage is only the most obvious of the many possible cases of this. Nevertheless, although sometimes the effect of one factor will be to determine positively or negatively the nature of the other, many different permutations and combinations are possible. For example, the situation of kinship is compatible with a large number of possible attitudes.

What is the 'bond' which constitutes a relationship in the social services or the medical profession as we have them today? It could be said to consist, first, of the *formal rules*, legal and administrative, which govern the provision of health care and welfare. To take the case of the doctor and patient we find that in most countries the relationship between doctor and patient is partly constituted by government legislation laying down the legal rights and duties of doctor and patient. There may, for example, be legislation laying down in general or specific terms when a patient has a legal right to medical care, to hospitalization and so on. There may even be cases, perhaps of certain infectious disorders or certain psychiatric disorders, where the doctor has a duty to commit the patient to care against his wishes. In the latter case, the authority by which in England and Wales a person may be compulsorily detained in hospital obtains legally from the 1959 Mental Health Act of Parliament. The medical practitioners and mental welfare officers concerned have to be properly trained and duly authorized. Indeed, the mental welfare officer is specifically given protection in case of civil or criminal proceedings arising from the carrying out of any of these compulsory duties, provided he has not acted 'in bad faith or without reasonable care'. Whatever the details of legislation, however, it is clear that the bond which holds doctor and patient together is at least a legal one. The same considerations *mutatis mutandis* hold of the social worker/client relationship.

The bond is constituted, secondly, by rather vaguer sets of rules, or even of expectations, which doctors and patients, social workers and clients have of each other. Doctors and social workers often refer to this as the 'ethics' of their professions.

There are many different facets to this. For example, a patient or client has the assurance that a doctor or social worker will not take advantage of him with respect to any information which emerges about his private life: that there will be no gossip about medical conditions, social predicaments and so on. The medical profession is very strict about enforcing its own discipline on these matters. Reciprocally a doctor would expect a patient to tell the truth, to try to carry out prescribed treatment and so on. Social workers indeed go as far as to speak of a 'contract' between themselves and their clients.

What kinds of *attitude* should accompany these bonds? First of all, the caring worker ought to be *impartial*. This really follows from what we have said about equity. The caring worker is one of those in a position to distribute benefits in accordance with relevant criteria of need, desert and so on, and it would be unfair of him or her to show favouritism or prejudice in ignoring relevant differences or regarding irrelevant ones. In this sense the caring worker must have an *objective* attitude to his clients.

There is another kind of objective attitude which is *not* in general appropriate to clients or patients: that which incorporates the assumption that what they do is not, despite appearances, freely chosen by them but is governed by forces and factors over which they have no control.[10] Thus one may say to oneself 'She can't help lashing out at me like that, she's experiencing the change of life' or 'He obviously would marry very young, he's from a broken home', appealing not to any rational thought on the agent's part but to underlying causal factors seen as explaining the action. Instead of reacting spontaneously with hostility, disapproval, etc., as would be appropriate towards a person who is responsible for his actions, a stance of detachment is taken up based on the idea 'Of course, he can't help it'. We are tempted in ordinary life to do this to avoid the strain of fully 'reactive' encounters with other people.

Medical and social workers are particularly prone to the temptation to adopt this latter kind of objective attitude. For example, some social workers are apt to construe everything done by a client as manifesting the workings of subconscious complexes of one kind or another; others, of a different persuasion, see what he does as manifestations of alienation, of the class struggle, and so on. Again, medical workers tend to say 'You only want to do that, you only see things in that way because you're ill. When you're well, you'll see things quite differently.' In both cases the effect is to undercut the reasons the agent himself would give for his action or thought and replace them by mechanisms on which the caring worker is an expert. The motivation for doing this may be, as in private life, the wish to avoid reactive encounters. But the caring worker may have no ulterior motive and may simply believe that he knows more about why his client does things than the client himself can do. In either case, the implication is that the client is not to be regarded as a self-determining being who acts in pursuance of his own purposes.

It might be objected here that if we assume that such attitudes are *wrong*, we are begging the question against determinism, which is after all a widely held position. Now it is true that we wish to repudiate determinism, as we shall do in the next chapter, because it does not do justice in our basic convictions about human beings. But this is not the only reason for condemning the adoption of objective attitudes. Many determinists also would wish to reject an analysis of human action which made no reference to the wishes and purposes of the individual agent, and depicted him, not just as determined, but also as governed by forces outside his conscious control. For even those determinists who think that some forms of determinism can be reconciled with moral responsibility would have to admit that *this* form cannot be so reconciled.

It might now be asked why the adoption of this attitude by the caring professions, even if it *is* ill-founded, is such a bad thing: surely, it might be said, what matters is what the medical or social worker *does*, not what he thinks. But this objection will not hold water. For one thing, the adoption of this kind of attitude, where it is discovered by the patient or client, is in general *hurtful*; he is made to feel that he is not taken seriously as a person. (There are, of course, some clients or patients who are exceptions to this rule, who *want* to be seen as determined by forces outside their control so as to evade responsibility for misdemeanours.)

In addition, the adoption of this attitude by the caring professions must in any case affect their actions. One of the actions often performed by the caring professions is the giving of *advice*; and clearly the type of advice given to someone who is thought of as rational, able to take a point and be influenced by it, is different from the advice given to someone who is *not* thought of as rational. (Indeed in the latter case 'advice' is not really the correct word, since 'advice' by definition appeals to reason; 'persuasion' or 'propaganda' may be more suitable words.) On a more fundamental level, a belief that people are at bottom determined by factors which bypass their own reason undermines the basis for the respect for liberty which we expounded in an earlier section; for there is no particular reason to refrain from pressurizing someone against his will if one feels that the 'will' in question is not particularly his in the first place.

All this may well seem rather unreasonable to members of the caring professions. After all, they will say, we are dealing all the time with people who on any reckoning are governed to a more than average extent by non-rational factors. In the nature of the case, medical workers will be coping with the mentally ill, with people whose rationality is impaired as a by-product of physical illness or who are under the influence of drugs. Social workers, though less obviously concerned with this problem, will also often be dealing with those who are mentally ill or disturbed, or who have a 'personality defect' deriving from childhood deprivation or the like. In these cases, it will be said, the second kind of objective attitude is surely *correct*. This is broadly true, but two points have to be borne in mind. First, there is always a temptation, which must be guarded against, to extend this kind of attitude beyond those people, and those aspects of people, which would justify it. The temptation exists because adopting this kind of objective attitude is often an easier option. Second, it may be profitable to adopt a reactive attitude even in some cases which may not justify it. The policy of treating people as rational unless proved otherwise may have the effect of fostering rationality, which is not an all-or-nothing matter.

A third attitude, or rather perhaps absence of attitude, which is often commended for caring workers is that they should be *non-judgmental*.[11] But the claim that caring workers should not be judgmental, though it is often advanced, is neither unambiguous nor uncontroversial. Let us examine some possible senses of it.

First of all, it might be maintained that a caring worker's job is always to help his client to what the *client* wants – whether relief of need or of suffering or whatever – and never to stand in his way. We might call this the *laissez-faire* interpretation of non-judgmentalism. As an absolute claim it cannot be sustained, for reasons we have already made clear in the section on respect for liberty; the medical or social worker is restricted by his duties to other people, whether these are statutory duties, such as those to report notifiable diseases or to carry out the terms of a proba- tion order, or a general duty to protect others from harm, as when for example there is a suspicion that a child is being 'battered'. But, as we saw earlier, there is an obligation not to interfere beyond what is required by the rights of others.

Second, it might be maintained that the caring worker should refrain from *forming* moral judgments on his clients' character and actions. This claim is in itself ambiguous. It might mean, on the one hand, that clients should be regarded as not responsible, not suitable subjects for moral assessment. Now there are doubt- less some clients with respect to whom such a maxim would be sound, in so far as they are not reasonably to be held responsible for their actions. But to extend this idea to all clients would be to regard them with the wrong kind of objective attitude and to rob them of all dignity. On the other hand, the claim may be that caring workers should not always be mentally *raising the question* as to their clients' moral score and assessing their moral standing. The temptation to keep a tally in this way arises in those aspects of social work where what first brought the client into the scope of social work is a crime or failing which may be regarded as a moral as well as a legal fault. But a client can legitimately feel that his *moral* standing, where it is to be distinguished from his public obligations, is between him and his Maker (or whatever is the secular equivalent of that idea). A social worker has no more business to be taking his moral temperature than that of any other member of the community; and to assume otherwise is to take on a quasi-parental role of responsibility for another's soul which is almost as lacking in respect for his capacity for self-determination as the wrong kind of objective attitude.

The social worker might well retort, however, that although we should not always be keeping a moral score of others' progress *some* measure of moral assessment of other people is unavoidable, and indeed a natural consequence of having moral principles one- self. People, including one's client, sometimes *provoke* moral judgment by their conduct, and the same applies to the medical worker's patients. This is so, but in these cases the caring worker has the same duty of fairness to his clients as to others: he must ask himself what mitigating circumstances there are, whether he himself given those circumstances would have done any better, whether he is damning a whole person on one action, whether the principle in terms of which he is judging is beyond question, and so on.

The third way in which it is said that a caring worker should not be judgmental concerns the *expressing* of moral opinions, as distinct from merely forming them. We may distinguish here between those cases where the moral matter comes within the scope of the caring worker and those where it does not. In the latter sphere the caring worker cannot, by definition, speak with any authority borrowed from his role, and so the issue is the same as the issue of whether any lay person may pronounce on moral questions. The usual view would be that he may certainly pronounce in the same way as anyone else if asked, or even unasked where the matter is of great importance to someone else's welfare, but that it would be officious to criticize beyond this, for example, to say 'It was dishonest of you to tell those neighbours that your telly is out of order and they can't come and watch it.'

Of course the more common case is that of moral issues which arise within the caring worker's sphere of competence. He may have a duty, not as caring worker but simply as moral agent, to speak out and indeed to intervene if someone is being ill-treated: this was discussed under the heading of liberty (see p.57). But there is a nebulous area where the matter is by no means so clear-cut, where the client is behaving in a more generally thoughtless or feckless manner (as the caring worker sees it): spending welfare money on foolish luxuries, allowing the house and children to descend into needless squalor, impairing health by over-indulgence, and so on. Here the caring worker has to consider and balance various competing factors. First, the 'failings' of the client may be of a kind to strain public resources in the long term, and if so the worker can and should speak as agent of the welfare services, expressing not his personal disapproval but his 'official' view as disburser of public money. Second, however, the client is an independent moral agent, with his own views about what matters, and has therefore a right to toleration from the worker where it does not interfere with others. Third and on the other hand again, the worker has his own standards;

and whereas standards do not require to be declared on every occasion, they logically must set limits on what the worker can be called upon actively to endorse, as with those doctors and nurses who have conscientious objections to abortion.

A fourth attitude which all caring workers ought to have is *compassion*. It might be thought that they logically must have this attitude, in virtue of their jobs. But this is not so: a person can take on a caring job for various *extrinsic* reasons, as we saw earlier. And even a caring worker who is basically interested in the intrinsic aims of his or her profession can lose sight of compassion in the day-to-day dealings with clients: for example, a doctor who is passionately concerned with the relief of misery and suffering may still speak brusquely and insensitively to a patient. What is morally required, then, is a kind of steady maintenance of the awareness that the other party has the capacity to suffer: an attitude which is in fact morally required of all of us, but which is especially vital to the caring worker who is constantly among people in trouble.

It is often said that the caring worker should have a *personal* relationship with his clients. Is this characteristic of personalness a fifth component in the ideal attitude of the caring worker? It might seem from what we have been saying as though personalness, so far from being desirable, is logically *incompatible* with the caring worker's situation. We have said that the caring worker has a role-relationship or business relationship with his client which is structured and formalized in terms of certain rights and duties both officially laid down and unofficially understood. Because of this formal structure, the role-relationship does not concern all aspects of the participants' lives and deals with people not as particular unique individuals but as falling into certain categories: sufferers from certain diseases, claimants for particular kinds of benefit and so on. By contrast, a personal relationship is not formally structured. Potentially, at least, it involves all aspects of the lives of the participants, and it is concerned with individuals as particular, unique persons: if A is in love with B, for example, A has a feeling for B as an *individual*, not as exemplifying characteristics which others might share, and his feeling is by definition concerned with one person *rather* than others.

These considerations are true as far as they go of caring relationships in contemporary society. But they do not provide

a definitive answer to the question of whether caring relationships should be personal. For it could be maintained that the
structure of rights and duties should be *replaced* by a personal
relationship or that personal relationships should be developed
alongside the role-relationship. Let us consider each of these
points in turn.

It is not easy to see how the structure of rights and duties could
be *replaced* as long as caring workers are professionals who are
paid by someone, whether the payer is the State, the client or a
charitable body. For someone who is paid to do a job is in a
structure of rights and duties in virtue of that very fact. Nor is it
easy to envisage the possibility of non-professional medical
workers, except fringe workers who practise amateur group
therapy, meditation and the like. Of course we have had a society
with amateur, unpaid social workers. But if these are Victorian-
style Lady Bountifuls they do not introduce a personal relationship; and if they are friends and neighbours doing a good turn
their ministrations, though obviously desirable in themselves, are
too haphazard to replace the social work system completely, as we
saw earlier.

Perhaps, then, it is possible for caring workers to build personal
relationships alongside the role-relationships in which they are
placed *vis-à-vis* their clients. This is not a logical contradiction:
employer and employee, teacher and pupil, *can* also be friends or
lovers. But is it psychologically possible, and in any case is it
desirable? Some things are clearly not psychologically possible. A
caring worker cannot be in love with all his clients. Nor can he
even like them all: in saying this we mean not only that liking is
involuntary, but also that it is a matter of individual *taste*, and it is
therefore bound to discriminate between clients. But there are
ways in which a caring worker's attitude might be personal or
friend-like. For example, he can show that *intensity* of concern for
and emotional involvement in his clients' welfare which is more
commonly found in personal relationships. Again, he can take
special note of individual differences between clients and their
situations. Again, he can adopt an informal *manner*, as when young
doctors call elderly women patients 'Granny'. Again, he can take
an interest in aspects of clients' lives which are outside his particular official concern with them. In all these ways a caring worker
can behave *like* a friend, and see himself as offering friendship.

The *desirability* of behaving like a friend, however, needs further consideration. Taking note of individual differences – regarding everyone as an individual, not a 'case' – is necessary for good caring. It is true that the doctor's professional interest is in a patient *as* a sufferer from a particular kind of cancer, or whatever; but not all sufferers from a particular condition are the same, even in their physiological reactions, let alone their emotional attitudes, their social background, their moral principles. If the doctor is to make a success of dealing with the patient, with due regard for his liberty, with real compassion, and so on, he has to regard him as an individual. In the same way the social worker is dealing, not just with a *case* of juvenile fire-raising or pensioner's penury, but with individuals who come into his province for these reasons. As we shall see in the next chapter, this feature of caring work requires an insight going beyond the categories of science and social science.

Caring workers are often warned against getting too involved with clients. But presumably genuine compassion *entails* a measure of involvement, and the sense of someone caring is welcomed by clients who are friendless. The obverse of this coin – being personally involved – is that the caring worker is sometimes justified in getting angry. If he is really being 'messed about' – told lies, or given promises which are clearly insincere, for example – anger would be entirely appropriate, as indeed it can sometimes be appropriate with shopkeepers and others with whom the relationship is clearly one of business only. To assume it is *never* appropriate, that clients must always be let off a natural human reaction to being badly treated, is to adopt the undesirable form of objective attitude.

An informal manner would be welcomed by some clients in some contexts though it makes some tasks (for example, attempts to impose any necessary authority) more difficult. Similarly, many clients would welcome the taking of a *general* interest in their lives. The danger in both cases is that the social worker will be seen to be invading privacy and forcing friendship – after all, people in normal circumstances *choose* their friends. Moreover, as we have seen, this 'friendship' is really friend-like behaviour – befriending – and any attempt to portray it as something else is 'phony'. But the value of befriending must not be under-estimated. For the lonely and helpless, befriending can be a lifeline; and the realization that the relationship is not one of ordinary friendship need not inhibit it. We might indeed say that there are really *two* kinds of relationship which may be called personal. The first kind is *exclusive*, like that between friends proper or lovers; the caring worker cannot have this kind of personal relationship with all his clients. The second kind, however, is potentially *all-embracing*; it is simply that response to another person as an individual which forms the basis of all real compassion and concern.

We have been discussing caring relationships on the basis of the Welfare State as we have it at present. The question with which we began this section concerned the difference between caring relationships in such a state and in a market economy. Can we now say that the Welfare State rectifies a *fault* of the market state, namely that in the latter caring relationships are merely business ones? As we have seen, the difference between market and welfare states is certainly not that in the latter type of state caring relationships lose their *rule-governed* quality. On the contrary, social work at least is *less* rule-governed in a market state, in that there it is largely done, if at all, by volunteers; and is in many ways the worse for that, as we have suggested. It is true, however, that in a welfare state the relationship between caring worker and client is not a direct *commercial* relationship, as it is in the market state. This contrast applies mainly to medical care, since there is not a proper commercial equivalent to the social worker. So the question becomes: is the relationship between medical worker and patient better in a welfare state than in a market state, given that it will be rule-governed in either case but will not be commercial in the Welfare State?

The answer surely is that it may not make any difference. Certainly, a commercial relationship, if looked at purely in the abstract, is what we have called 'non-tuistic'. But no actual relationship will be as simple as this. Alongside the commercial aspect of the situation can flourish the impartiality, compassion and personal attention which we have been commending. It is true that the unscrupulous private doctor can look on a patient simply as one more fee; but similarly the unscrupulous NHS doctor can look on a patient as one more capitation fee. In either case the extrinsic aim of the worker may be to make money. As a matter of historical fact, more people probably felt they had a personal relationship with their doctor in 'the old days'. But if this is so, it does raise the question whether the greater centralization and bureaucratization natural in a welfare state are inimical to good caring relationships. Let us then conclude this section by considering the advantages and disadvantages of this institutionalization of caring work.

The advantages are the protections which an organized body can give to both worker and client. Such a body can protect clients by laying down sanctions against workers who abuse confidentiality or go beyond their rights to intervene, and can also help and protect workers in various ways. For instance, it is good for all professions to have ways and means whereby new skills and knowledge can be shared, and in general whereby members of a profession can support and encourage each other. Again, doctors and social workers require legal or similar professional protection from exploitation, unfair criticism or legal action against them by their patients and clients. There must also be some institutional mechanism whereby the professions can criticize themselves and look for ways of improving their services to the public, protecting them from quacks and so on.

There are also aspects of institutionalization which are not conducive to good caring relationships. In the first place, a strong institutional framework can encourage resistance to change within a profession. This is partly because rules and hierarchies establish habits of thought and behaviour with their own inertia, partly because large institutions develop their own salaried or unsalaried officials who have vested interests in resisting radical changes. Second, institutions develop a firm identity and a clear view of what is and is not their proper province. In industry there is the familiar problem of the demarcation dispute, and in like manner in medicine there is the problem of what is or is not a medical matter. The dangers here are now to a limited extent being recognized and health centres may have social workers on call. But it may be that what the patient needs is not another 'expert', but a wider or more personal relationship with his doctor. In this matter the medical profession may be drifting away from the ideals and practices of a previous generation. No doubt there are many causes of this, but one cause is the move away from the ideal of medicine as a *vocation* to that of medicine as a *profession*, with the professional concomitants of institutional structure and hierarchy. Third, along with the development of an institutional structure goes a professional exclusiveness. Once again, it is easy to see a good side to this: the emphasis on rigorous training and so on. But we also see suspicion of other professions, like social work, which might be thought to be poaching, contempt for what is called 'fringe medicine', even in areas where orthodox medicine has made little progress, and a determination to retain an exclusive right to prescribe even mild drugs. Along with professional exclusiveness goes, fourth, an undue concern with status, with maintaining the prestige and remuneration of the profession.

The advantages and disadvantages of a strong institutional structure in a profession are illustrated also in social work. In their struggle to develop professional expertise, to gain social approval, to safeguard their clients' interests, to be treated as equals by other professions, social workers have developed a powerful institutional structure with a conception of professional ethics and many other characteristic features. The advantages of this institutional structure are clear, but the same problems arise: an undue emphasis on 'expertise', a 'distancing' from the client, professional exclusiveness, concern with status and so on. And none of these factors contribute to the development of better caring relationships, any more than do the economic bonds of buying and selling.

There is indeed a paradox in this. In order to overcome, or at least to mitigate, the effect of a *laissez-faire* market state the Welfare State was introduced in Britain. But the Welfare State required a vast army of professionals in all the health and social services, and the more professional, the more 'expert' they became, the more they approximated to a vast state bureaucracy, and thus the less effective they became in fostering the personal caring relationships thought to be lacking in the *laissez-faire* state. But some of these difficulties belong to over-centralization, rather than to the Welfare State as such, and recently there have been efforts to move back towards a less centralized system.

The sense of community

A fifth criticism which may be made of the *laissez-faire* market economy is that it cannot cater sufficiently for the notion of *community*. This criticism is not one but two: that the market economy can have no conception of the public good or interest, and that the market economy inhibits the growth of fellow-feeling and fraternity throughout the community. We shall consider each of these criticisms in turn.

To explain the notion that the market system cannot have a concern for the public good, let us consider the topical example of environmental pollution from industrial waste. Some firms might be prepared to meet the extra costs involved in preventing pollution, but are afraid that competitors might not follow their example and that they would on that account be at a disadvantage in the market. The point here is that while we can perhaps agree that the economic relation is also a juridical relation without departing from the tradition of Adam Smith, issues such as pollution and its prevention raise moral considerations which go beyond enforcement of contract and the like. If we do think that the economic-juridical relation should be enlarged to include matters such as pollution we are operating with hazy conceptions of a public interest and of a continuing community. Neither of these conceptions fits very easily into Adam Smith's tradition of individualism and hedonism.

At this point it might be said that defenders of a market system often assume that the long-term public interest will in fact result from each individual's pursuit of his own interest. In the work of Adam Smith this idea is expressed in terms of the 'invisible hand' which harmonizes all interests, and when he first uses this idea it has a religious connotation, that of a benevolent God who will order all things well. But whether because God does not work in this way, or because there is no God, it does not always seem to be *true* that long-term public interest results from the pursuit of individual interest.

If the market system cannot accommodate a concern for the public interest, it is not clear that the concern for social justice typical of the welfare services generates it either. The reason is that an adequate analysis of public or community interest requires the use of concepts which cannot be reduced to ideas about the interests of individuals, whereas the concern for social justice is pre-eminently the concern for the interests of existing individuals. To say this, of course, is not to commit oneself to any metaphysical view about the existence of a special entity, 'the public', over and above the individuals who make up the public. Moreover, to argue that the good of the public is not just that of the individuals of whom at any given time the public consists is not to suggest that a government may impose some conception of intrinsic good with no relation to what individuals within the society actually want. The point is rather that a government must develop the implications of what the public at a given time actually want in order to elicit an enlightened conception of what in the long run they will want. The furtherance of the public good may therefore result in policies or interventions by a government which produce no immediate benefit for anyone. It seems to us that some such idea of the good or interest of a continuing community is involved in support for (for example) anti-pollution legislation, and while it is not clear that such an idea can be accommodated in the individualistic and hedonistic tradition of a free market economy, it equally has no place in the programmes of social justice typical of welfare legislation. The reason is that such an idea involves a concern not with achieving justice between *competing* interests but with serving a *unified* interest; and also perhaps with fostering some ideals of what our way of life *ought* to be like in the future and what is worth preserving in it.

The other aspect of the criticism that the market state is hostile to the sense of community is the charge that it is inimical to the growth of fellow-feeling or fraternity in the community. The ground for this charge is that the inequalities resulting from its emphasis on competition lead to deep divisions between 'haves' and 'have-nots' or between workers and bosses, with resulting hostility or at best estrangement. But the fraternity which is sought by these critics of the market society is not simply an automatic by-product of equality, for any arrangement which keeps people in separate compartments, even if equality is achieved, is still said to be inimical to the feeling that we are 'all members one of another'. (Thus people criticize any version of *apartheid*, however equitable, on the ground that it destroys fraternity.) On this kind of view, then, the advantage of the Welfare State is not merely that it promotes greater equality which is conducive to fraternity, but also that it involves the majority of people in one system of education, health, housing and so on – an arrangement which strengthens cohesiveness in itself.

This whole question of fraternity, however, is immensely complicated. It is true by definition that a state in which people all take part in the same caring system is more *integrated*. But whether the people in such a state must *feel* more bound up in concern for a common welfare is another question. Moreover, it is really a psychologist's question rather than a philosopher's question. It is true that the Welfare State aims at lessening inequalities, and in so far as these breed hostility the result of lessening them should be greater overall fraternity. But one must set against that the unifying power of *enmity* – it may be that there is a brotherhood of those who feel oppressed, and another of those who feel threatened by the first group, which is more intense that anything which can be achieved by a larger group not united by any common enemy. Moreover, there are three ways in which the creation of a welfare state may actually militate *against* the development of fraternity in the community. First, it may make people feel that there is no longer any need for any private concern for one's neighbour – 'they' can now be relied upon to do everything. Second – and this is a consequence of the professionalization of social work – ordinary people may come to feel that they do not have the expertise needed to help with family or personal difficulties. Third – and this again arises from the inward-looking institutionalization of the caring services – a new division may arise, not between the 'haves' and the 'have-nots', but between the caring workers and those worked upon: a division which may incidentally promote a fraternity among the 'victims', but not of the kind intended.

The cure for all these possible ills of the Welfare State is the same: the caring workers must abandon their isolation and begin to work *through* the community rather than *on* it. This is already happening to some extent. For example, community social workers aim to get people to help each other rather than doing the helping themselves *de haut en bas*. Again, there is greater stress than there was on community medicine, which is educative and preventive, trying to get people to look after their own health as far as they can. These movements help to rectify the anti-fraternal aspects of the Welfare State, and also play their part in counterpoising the quest for equality and the good of each with the pursuit of ideals and the good of all.

The State and the provision of health care

To illustrate some of the points we have been making in more detail, we shall now consider more fully the question of how health care should be provided. We shall find that the arguments all tend to involve a fine balancing of competing values and that in the end it is difficult to emerge with any very clear conclusion, especially as empirical issues are closely interwoven with moral ones.[12]

We saw earlier that a purely *laissez-faire* system of government is morally defective as a way of ensuring the health and welfare of *individuals* in the community (however adequate it may be as a system for ensuring *public health*). If that is accepted, we can now turn to other systems which are considered more plausible at the moment. Our strategy will be to mention first some of the advantages people have advanced in favour of what we shall call 'liberal humanitarianism', and the criticisms made of it from a socialist point of view. Then we shall turn to the advantages and disadvantages of socialism. Finally in this section we shall touch on the vexed and topical question of liberal *versus* pure socialism.

The liberal humanitarian system of health care is a modification of the *laissez-faire* system. As with the *laissez-faire* system, those who can afford it pay for themselves. But the needy are looked after not by private charity but by the State, using funds obtained by taxing the less needy. The first advantage attributed to the liberal humanitarian scheme is that it meets everyone's needs with minimum coercion: people are constrained only to the extent of paying taxes for the needy and not made to contribute to their own good, a practice which smacks of unwarranted interference. Second, it is said that resources are more usefully distributed: state aid can be concentrated on those who really need special help, and those who are paying for their own services will have an incentive not to squander them which they do not have under a state scheme.

The third and fourth advantages of the liberal humanitarian scheme are what may be called moral, rather than merely medical. The third is the advantage of preserved incentive. People are encouraged to work harder if they can get what they need only by working, and discouraged if extra work brings no extra reward. Having an incentive to work hard is a double advantage: it benefits the community by increasing prosperity and it cultivates industriousness in the individual's character. The fourth advantage is similarly one of development of character: to have to decide for oneself how to manage such an important department of one's life develops a sense of responsibility and powers of decision.

In criticizing this system, the socialist can first point to the problem posed for the liberal humanitarian by those who are perfectly well able to provide for themselves, by means of private insurance, but neglect to do so. If they fall ill even the liberal humanitarian will have to admit that the State must look after them; it is unfair that they should receive this benefit without paying for it, but one cannot leave a man to die because he has been improvident. The socialist can say that for him there is no problem, because everyone has to pay his way.

The second socialist criticism is a denial that the medical needs of the average man can in fact be met by a non-coercive liberal scheme, on the ground that the average man, not just the needy man, could not afford to pay for modern medicine individually, even if he had in his control all that part of his money which at present the State takes from him for general medical care. This assertion, if true, would be a knock-down argument against liberal humanitarianism. We shall not discuss it in detail, as it depends on economic rather than philosophical arguments. One point in its favour is that the distinction on which the liberal humanitarian scheme really rests, between being and not being too poor to buy necessities, does not apply to medical care even roughly, because one person's basic necessities in medical care may be vastly more expensive than another person's luxuries. There may therefore be those who, although quite well off, will not be able to afford, or even necessarily afford the premiums to cover, what is medically necessary for them. At best, then, a scheme which really meets people's needs will require state subsidies not merely for the poorest but also for the illest; and this is already a departure from the basic liberal humanitarian scheme. Apart from this, the question whether a private system would be cheap enough for the consumer depends on such things as the way in which, and scale on which, it is organized, the level of doctors' fees in such a system, and so on. We shall deal with the latter question shortly.

The third criticism is that to have some people recipients of state aid when the majority are paying for themselves creates an unfortunately sharp division between 'haves' and 'have-nots', the independent and the dependent, which is more blurred when all are in a state scheme. However strongly one might insist on the human right to medical care, those who are given it without paying, when others have to pay, will feel they are recipients of charity; and this feeling is damaging to self-esteem, and embittering to those who cannot help their dependent position.

The fourth socialist criticism of liberal humanitarianism is the most important and the most baffling, since it combines many different strands. It can be expressed by saying that the scheme makes medical care a commercial matter, and this is unsuitable. But why might it be thought to be unsuitable? Medicine is not like love, which logically cannot be bought. People say here that it is wrong to 'traffick in', or to 'exploit', people's need. This description might, however, apply equally well to those who sell food, or any needed commodity, and no one suggests that they are immoral; a butcher or baker meets a need and in doing so meets his own needs too, as Adam Smith points out (see p.71). There is, all the same, a difference in the medical case, which means that what may be called market safeguards do not protect the patient as well as they do the ordinary consumer. In general, the consumer is not actually suffering, as distinct from needy, and also he understands something of what he is buying; so he can 'shop around' and look for cheap goods and services. But a patient will not want to wait and will not know how to judge, so he can very easily be exploited. Nor would an agreed 'professional fee' system improve his position; on the contrary, if such fees were fixed at an excessive rate (as is perhaps the case with lawyers now) he would have no chance of finding the most favourable price for medical care.

The liberal humanitarian can agree with all these views, but points out that they do not constitute a special difficulty for his scheme as opposed to a socialist one. Given the urgency with which medical care is needed, doctors on a socialist scheme can also blackmail the consumers (here society at large) to pay them too much, so that again everyone suffers. The patient, he will argue, is best safeguarded by a private system, which will at least leave some room for 'shopping around'; apart from that he is protected by the compassion and goodwill of the majority of the profession.

Here, however, the socialist tends to retort that the market system implicit in the liberal humanitarian scheme is deficient precisely in that it leaves no room for compassion or goodwill. Those partaking in a market economy (he goes on) are in business to make a profit, and as large a one as possible, just as the consumer is trying to pay as little as possible: that is what the market is all about. Greed, then, rather than compassion, is the motive of the doctor in a liberal humanitarian scheme.

This socialist doctrine is, however, a muddle. It is true that what we may call a pure market transaction can be defined as one in which each party seeks to do as well as possible. But this is an artificial abstraction from actual practice, where what goes on might be a product of all kinds of forces; doctor and patient will both be governed by many non-market considerations in arriving at a fee. It is also true as a matter of fact that the doctor in commercial medicine must make enough to live on if he is to remain in business; so the bottom end of his scale is fixed. But there is no practical necessity for him to be a pure marketeer, trying to make the largest possible profit, and therefore no reason why his main motive should not be compassion just as much as if he had private means and worked for nothing. Nor does compassion for a person's sufferings entail refusal to take any money from him, any more than sympathy for a stranded motorist entails refusal to accept payment for a gallon of petrol. Of course a doctor in a *laissez-faire* system has a problem if his patients are too poor to pay enough even to support him. But in a liberal humanitarian system such patients are subsidized by the State.

We think then that the claim that medicine should not be a commercial matter cannot be sustained in its crude form. But there is nevertheless a difficulty about commercial medicine which arises less obviously in a socialist system: considerations of cost, rather than of need, will obtrude too much into the doctor's medical thinking. Of course the National Health Service doctor also is constantly being urged to economize. But if he thinks a certain expensive drug or treatment is needed for a patient, not merely useful or beneficial, he can go ahead. With a private patient, however, he will have to think all the time, 'Can this patient afford it?' and this must be very inhibiting to the process of making a balanced decision on treatment.

The strengths of the socialist position will already have emerged to some extent through their criticisms of the liberal humanitarian: a socialist scheme can offer very large resources to any individual who needs expensive treatment, in a way which avoids both the stigma suffered by the involuntary non-contributor and the unfair advantages enjoyed by the negligent one. It is also said that a socialist scheme avoids the self-interested motivation of a commercial scheme. But as we have seen there is no need for doctors participating in a commercial scheme to do so out of self-interest. Moreover, there is no reason why doctors, and patients, should not be self-interested within a state scheme: patients wanting more than their share of attention, doctors wanting more and more money. No doubt the philosophy behind the socialist scheme is 'from each according to his capacity, to each according to his need' – a kind of fraternal spirit. But there is nothing in the system to ensure that participants in fact see it this way. No doubt they can see their National Insurance contributions and taxes as benefiting the community rather than themselves; but then the liberal humanitarian can see his taxes in that way too.

It is also maintained in favour of a socialist system that it ensures equal treatment for equal needs. This unqualified claim is probably rather optimistic. On a socialist scheme influence, aggressiveness and articulateness will to some extent win more attention and care than is fair, just as money may do on a commercial scheme. But to claim an advantage over liberal humanitarianism on grounds of equality the socialist has only to show that his scheme has more equal results than the liberal alternative; and this he can probably do.

The question does arise, however, what importance is to be attached to achieving equality if everyone's basic needs are met; it might be maintained that above the level of basic needs the demands of equality are rather controversial. The real issue, then, is whether a socialist system meets people's needs more satisfactorily than its rivals. We have seen that where a large expenditure for one person is concerned this may be the case. But many would maintain that a socialist system is necessarily too wasteful of resources to be able to give a satisfactory routine service to all, on the grounds that the removal of any need to pay at the time encourages over-extravagant use. How far this common charge is borne out in practice is a question for the sociologist rather than for the philosopher, but it should be noted that 'unnecessary' calls upon the doctor's time are often due to ignorance rather than to selfishness: an educated person does not think of calling in a doctor for a cold or 'flu or bleeding nose, not because he is too public-spirited, but because he himself knows what to do. It should therefore be possible for the socialist to lessen abuses without needing the deterrent of payment, by educating the public rather more; and doctors nowadays seem to be far more willing to do this than they sometimes were in the past.

We suggest, then, that the socialist might be able to escape the charge that his system is necessarily inefficient. But there are two other charges that are perhaps even more serious: that a socialist scheme is an unwarranted infringement of liberty, and that it undermines individual responsibility. The first charge, however, is not so easy to maintain as some of those who make it seem to think. Obviously the scheme is a curtailment of liberty; but it would presumably be justified nevertheless if it promoted a great common good that could be achieved in no other way. The issue of liberty, then, is partly the issue of whether the alternative liberal humanitarian system is economically viable. But even if it were, we must still ask whether the unhappiness of those who are stigmatized under it is a price worth paying for retaining greater freedom. And to this there is no easy answer.

The second criticism is that socialized medicine undermines individual responsibility for health. In a socialist system, it may be said, the State takes over that responsibility for health care which under a private system the individual possesses: the need to plan how his health care (and that of his family) is to be paid for, and to decide his priorities accordingly. Why is this said to be a bad thing? Many reasons are advanced. One is that the individual will come to think that all aspects of health care are now looked after by Them, and so cease to take responsibility for those things which on any system only he can provide: a sensible diet, adequate sleep and so on. Whether this happens in fact is an empirical question; it seems to us likely that those people who do take this kind of responsibility for themselves are too individualistic to be affected one way or the other.

A second reason for criticizing the removal of responsibility is that it trivializes the individual's concern for his life: the more the important areas of life are taken over by government, the more people see their main business in life as the contriving of amusement. Instead of thinking about health and education, they think about clothes and holidays. Now this is perhaps a tendentious description of the situation, as we saw in the third section of this chapter: if one were to say that state control of the utilities of life gives people more chance to cultivate their talents and develop their personal relationships, to think about things worthwhile in themselves rather than merely useful, the argument against state control would be less clear. But perhaps most people's capacity to achieve the aristocratic ideal of leisure, as opposed to mere amusement, is limited; if so, it might in general be true that too much socialism leads people to give trivial things undue importance in life.

The third and most important argument advanced against this kind of removal of responsibility is the claim that it saps character. On a liberal humanitarian scheme people have to make decisions and live with the results of them, whereas on a socialist scheme decisions are taken out of their hands. The argument is that a person who does not have to make decisions cannot express his individuality, because it is in making one's own choices, different from anyone else's, that individuality is both shown and fostered; and moreover he loses some of that capacity for self-determination which makes him a person in the full sense.

The socialist can reply that these considerations apply unqualifiedly only when every area of life is governed by the State; the nationalization of some aspects of life, such as education, housing and health, leaves plenty of scope for individual choice and decision. He might admit that there is even so a measure of deterioration in character, but think it amply compensated for by the increased benefits; or he might take the line that there is no need to assume that people's characters suffer at all. But even if he is right in this latter claim about what actually happens, the liberal can object on moral grounds: even supposing that character remains intact in a socialist world, is it appropriate to treat adults as though they were children, capable of deciding only unimportant matters? This is where the liberty and responsibility arguments coincide; liberty, it might be said, is liberty in the exercise of responsibility. Treating people properly involves respecting their liberty, or treating them as responsible creatures. But, as we said earlier, even the claims of liberty may have to bow to those of utility, or those of humanity to those who would suffer under a libertarian scheme.

We come now to the final section of the discussion: the issue of pure *versus* liberal socialism. At present our own system is a liberal version which allows those who wish and are able to do so to buy extra services on a private basis, but many people now advocate that this should be forbidden by law and pure socialized medicine imposed. The issue is very complex. In Great Britain the question is whether people should be allowed to supplement the services they can get under the National Health Service. But there is also the possibility of a system whereby people can opt out of the National Health Service altogether. We cannot go into the pros and cons of this latter system. Again, even in Great Britain there are two separate questions: whether private medicine in state hospitals should be forbidden, and whether private medicine should be forbidden altogether. We shall not be able to distinguish between these two positions with the exactness which they really require. A further complexity is that the degree of extra service which is available for private purchase varies very much. We shall assume that it consists only of earlier appointments and more leisurely consultations with general practitioners and specialists, freer choice of specialist, prompter hospital treatment for non-emergencies and more privacy in hospital. Private treatment is not necessarily better in any respect other than these, and the degree to which it is better even in these will vary from place to place.

The usual argument concerns the right to private treatment. But we would suggest that for some people on some occasions private treatment may be not merely a right but a duty. Whatever the arguments against it, they can surely on occasion be morally outweighed, for those who can manage to afford private treatment, by obligations to others: the obligation to be restored to full health quickly and not be a drag on family or colleagues; the obligation to arrange a hospital stay at the least difficult time for family or colleagues; the obligation to continue working in hospital and to secure the privacy which makes this possible. The fact that not everyone can afford private medicine does not absolve those who can from this kind of duty. It would sometimes be true to say, contrary to the normal view, that a person who insisted on public medicine when he could afford private was being selfish and unpublic-spirited.

Of course the usual defence of private medicine is in terms not of duties but of rights. People have a right, it is said, to spend their money on what they like: some, it is often added, spend their spare money on bingo or drinking, why should I not spend mine on health insurance? This is basically an appeal to liberty. The mention of those who spend their money on smoking or drinking is an attempt to add considerations of equality. It is salutary to be reminded that there are now a great many ordinary people who could afford private treatment if they gave it high priority. But there are still some who could not, and while this is so, a man cannot claim the right to buy private treatment merely on grounds of equality. What he has to say instead is, why is it thought that people should be free to spend far more than the poorest can spend on every other kind of goods, but not on medical care?

One reply might be that people should not be free to spend unequally in any sphere: in other words, wealth should be redistributed equally. We have already refused to enter into discussion of this general question and suggested that what is uncontroversial and of paramount importance is the meeting of needs. But this is precisely why some people who are by no means egalitarians in general are against private medicine. The public system, they maintain, does not at present meet people's basic needs, especially their need of reasonably prompt treatment. The so-called 'extras' which private medicine provides are on this view not mere luxuries but basic necessities, open to the rich but too expensive for the poor. Assertions that we are free to buy everything other than medical care are thus beside the point, in so far as there is no other basic necessity beyond the reach of the poorest.

If this account is true, there are some medical necessities which can at present be got only by paying extra. But it does not follow that everyone's basic needs will more nearly be met if no one is allowed to pay extra. It is said that private patients use up a disproportionate amount of scarce resources; if they were done away with, queues would shorten and beds would multiply. But the extra services they receive are surely small in comparison with the extra money they pay; in other words, they are subsidizing other patients. Without their money, resources would therefore be scarcer and queues longer, especially as some doctors would leave the profession or the country if there were no private patients. We suggest then that private medicine may be one of those inequalities which are justified in that everyone, including the worst off, benefits from them.

The sensitive individual may still feel reluctant to avail himself of private medicine, even if he is convinced that the National Health Service can do with his money. We think this is to do with a sense of the fraternity of suffering: a wish not to cut oneself off from fellow-sufferers by having an easier time, even if one's easier time is of use to them. Such a feeling is certainly likeable, just as is a person's reluctance to eat his Christmas dinner when he thinks of those who are starving. But if we are right about the value of the private patient's contributions he should ignore his feelings on this matter.

In this section of the chapter we have been concerned with some of the systems of health care which follow from the assertion that, contrary to the political thinking of *laissez-faire*, government does have a positive duty towards assisting individuals in need. As always in real-life issues, the philosophical aspect is too intertwined with the empirical, and the empirical too elusive in any case, to permit any dogmatism. What we have hoped to do is simply to bring out some of the principles at issue in any discussion of the rights and wrongs of different systems of health care which are advocated in the name of the Welfare State.

Criteria for fixing the salaries of caring workers

In this section we shall consider the factors which have to be taken into account when an attempt is made to ascertain the proper level of salaries for caring workers, both in comparison with other groups of workers and within the various branches of the caring professions. We shall not attempt a detailed analysis of salary levels in the different branches of the professions, if only because such an analysis would very rapidly become out-of-date. Instead we shall consider some of the arguments used when salaries are discussed and try to assess their merits.

The phrase 'proper level of salary' needs a little explanation before we go further. In a purely market-governed economy, the proper level of salary for anyone (if indeed the phrase is appropriate at all in such a society) is simply what he can get in accordance with the laws of supply and demand. We are not, however, using the phrase merely in this sense, because we are going to take account of the notion that there is such a thing as a just or fair wage for a given job. On the other hand, we cannot ignore market considerations altogether. In fixing a wage, any employer has to consider whether he can get and keep sufficient workers at that wage, and this depends largely on whether they can do better elsewhere, financially or in other ways. It follows that sometimes it may be proper for social services to pay workers more than fairness would require if this is necessary for the maintenance of an adequate public service. We suggest, then, that the considerations to which appeal in the context of the social services is made fall into two broad types: considerations of fairness or justice, and considerations of utility or public interest. Both types of consideration can be employed to support judgments that one group *should* be or *ought* to be paid more or less than another group; but only considerations of justice can support judgments that one group has a *right* to more or less, since appeals to public interest are based, not on what is due to the person concerned, but on the good of everyone.

It will be seen that so far we are talking about *relative* claims, that one group should get more or less than another; and some such relativity is usually implied, if not stated, in discussions about the proper level of salary. But there can also be claims that a group is not paid enough in what appears to be an *absolute* sense, viz., enough to meet its basic needs. In general this kind of claim could not be made by caring workers, but it can be made with some plausibility by various groups of auxiliary hospital staff, so we shall discuss it briefly before turning to the more usual questions of relativities.

A claim based on basic needs can be seen in three ways. It might be maintained that we should out of compassion and charity relieve distress. Alternatively, it might be said, as we have seen earlier, that people have a *right* to a minimum standard of living, a right which talk of charity tends to obscure. But of course there are some communities so impoverished that it is impossible to give everyone even a minimum standard of living, and it is not clear that we can intelligibly speak of an absolute right to what may be impossible. Bearing this point in mind, we might say, thirdly, that people have an *equal* right to satisfaction of basic needs. What this means is that no one has a right to luxuries unless everyone has basic necessities. It is a minimally egalitarian claim, which asserts that there are some inequalities in provision, namely those which leave the worst-off below the level of basic needs, which cannot be justified.

This third way of looking at the claim of basic needs, since it is now expressed in *relative* terms after all, can definitely be seen as an aspect of justice: the claim is that it is *unfair* that some people can scarcely survive while others in the same community are prosperous. This version of the claim sounds more controversial than those expressed in terms of charity or human rights, since it maintains in effect that some people have too *much*. But it should be noted that it need not be based on the egalitarian premise, which some do not find intuitively obvious: its proponents can accept that there are grounds for justified differentiation, in terms of merit, desert and so on, and then reasonably ask whether differences in merit or desert are really so great as to justify differences in satisfaction on this scale.

Let us now return to our consideration of the factors to which appeal is normally made when *relativities* are discussed: in other words, when it is claimed that one group should get more or less than another. It will be recalled that we divided the factors into appeals to justice and appeals to utility, the latter consisting, broadly speaking, in considerations of the need, in the public interest, to provide *incentives*. Care is needed in distinguishing these two kinds of appeal, as the notion of *justifying* can be used in connection with either. Thus it might be said that higher salaries for consultants are *justified* on the utility ground that otherwise too many of them would emigrate. But if this were the *only* ground, we could not say that their higher salaries were just or fair, or that they had a right to them, any more than we say the hijacker has a right to the use of an aeroplane simply because it is in the public interest to give it to him.

We have written as though considerations of justice and of utility are entirely independent. But in fact they are related in two ways. First, the level of incentive needed to make people take on a disagreeable task is also a rough-and-ready measure of the disadvantages for which it is fair to compensate them: only rough-and-ready, because at a time of unemployment people may not need so much incentive to take on what is still a very disagreeable task, and because people can have prejudices which deter them from trying jobs which are not unpleasant in fact. Second, considerations of justice are among the factors which provide incentives or disincentives. Thus a man may decide to leave a job, or not to enter it, not just because he wants more money, but because he thinks it is *unfairly* remunerated.

What then are the various considerations of justice and utility used to justify differences in income? One such is *need*: not basic needs, but differences in other needs. One such difference is in *personal* position (number of dependents and so on). These differences are taken care of in our society, not by different salaries, but in the form of allowances and benefits, though presumably where the State is the employer it could make the difference in the pay itself. (It might of course be said that those with families have voluntarily incurred this 'need', just like anyone else who takes up an expensive hobby, and it is not fair that families should be supported where motor racing, say, is not. But the difference lies in the *utility* of subsidizing families, both from the point of view of the dependents themselves and the wider point of view of society.)

Another kind of difference in need is between the requirements of one *profession* and another. Social workers and doctors need cars, dentists need expensive equipment and so on. Members of these professions *need* to expend more than many people in order to earn their living, so it is fair that they should receive more. (It should be noted, however, that 'the requirements of a profession' are by no means uncontroversial. Does a doctor need, not merely *a* car, but a *smart* car to keep up 'the image of the profession'? Only if the profession cannot be practised without sustaining a certain kind of image.) Paying people more in so far as they *need* more is really producing equality at one remove. In effect, the inequality in payment is a means to an equality in satisfaction – assuming, that is, that payment is important only as a means to the satisfactions that can be bought by it.

The next ground for justifying differences in income is *amount of work done*. In so far as medical and social workers 'put in' longer hours, or more strenuous hours, than other workers, they *deserve* more pay. This is so intuitively natural that it needs no defence; but it perhaps needs an explanation. One idea behind it might be that effort morally deserves a reward; but that idea suggests that those who do not work as hard as medical and social workers are morally blameworthy, which does not seem right. A second idea rests on the notion that each person may be deemed to *own* his labour capacity, so that the more of it he sells the higher price he should be given in return. This is a very persuasive idea which certainly accounts for part of our thinking on the question. But it does not account for the principle of *overtime*, now being appealed to in awarding junior doctors' pay: the principle that longer hours should be paid not *pro rata* but at a higher rate than shorter hours. This principle can however be understood in terms of a third idea: that of *compensation*. According to this idea, work is unpleasant, and so the more of it one does the more one should be compensated, on a sort of 'equal satisfactions' principle. This idea may be too sweeping to apply to all work, but it is plausible to say that long and 'unsocial' hours can become a burden which should be compensated for by a higher rate, not merely paid for at a standard rate.

There are, of course, other aspects of medical and social work which bring in issues of compensation. Traditionally the kinds of feature which call for compensation are 'dirt' and danger. Both these are relevant in some degree to medicine: doctors and nurses (perhaps especially nurses) have to handle nauseating wounds and other unpleasant things, and run a risk of infection. Social workers in general are in some danger from violent criminals and mentally unstable people, and police and prison officers are especially vulnerable.

So far we have considered compensation and fair prices for amount of labour simply from the point of view of justice. But clearly utility also demands a higher wage for long and arduous jobs. If people feel that they are being asked to shoulder special burdens without due compensation, they will tend to go into other jobs and the community will not get enough nurses, prison officers and so on. This does not mean that such inequalities in pay are just because they benefit everyone, as some philosophers have suggested. They are *useful* because they benefit everyone, and are justified partly on that ground. But they are *just*, if at all, because they represent a fair return to the recipient for his extra and sometimes burdensome labour. The distinction between considerations of justice and those of utility are relevant when people say that making nurses, for example, or social workers too well-off will attract the wrong people into the professions. If this were true, and if utility were the only factor to be considered, we *should* pay our social workers and nurses meagrely. But just as important as utility is justice – fair return for the type of work.

Another factor often considered in fixing differentials is *responsibility*. Responsibility is relevant to the caring professions in two ways: first, the professions as a whole involve greater responsibility for people's lives and welfare than many professions (though perhaps not more so than many quite humble occupations, e.g. that of a railway signalman); second, there can be greater and smaller degrees of responsibility *within* the professions.

That greater responsibility of both these kinds should be rewarded is often thought of as obvious. But the basis of this idea is not in fact very clear. One ground is said to be a utilitarian ground, to do with status: people are apt to revere money and what it can buy, and so someone known to have more money finds it easier to impose authority, as those with responsibility need to do. But people's reverence for money is rather ambiguous: are social workers more revered than they were, now that they are paid at a more competitive rate? In any case, this argument about status would not show that it is *just* to pay people for responsibility, as would usually be maintained.

There are two ways in which payment for responsibility can be linked with justice rather than utility. The first way is via the idea of *compensation*: responsibility is an unpleasant burden which people ought to be rewarded for undertaking. Now of course some assumptions of responsibility involve extra work in any case. There is no problem about seeing these in terms of compensation. It is also said that the anxiety attendant on having to make important decisions is itself a burden. But this seems to us rather controversial. For some people, and for everyone on some occasions, this is undoubtedly true; but it is also true that there are people who thrive on the feeling that their decisions are important – it is the impotence and frustration of *lack* of responsibility which these people find a burden. It is also notorious that in the caring professions, as elsewhere, those in positions of extra responsibility tend to *escape* some of the more straightforwardly burdensome aspects of the job: night-work, visiting in slums, etc. So far, then, we would cast doubt on the idea that responsibility purely as such should be highly paid.

It will no doubt be objected that there are good utilitarian reasons for paying people more to assume positions of responsibility: namely, that otherwise not enough people will be willing to do so. But this objection presupposes that responsibility is in fact unpleasant, which is what we have been concerned to deny. It will also be said that unless we pay people to assume responsibility the only people who will assume it are power-hungry undesirables. But as it is, we might reply, people assume responsibility for the sake of extra money rather than because they feel they are suitable candidates. This whole question is of course largely an empirical one; philosophy can only question the assumptions in this field, not settle the issues.

The other way in which payment for responsibility can be seen as a matter of justice is in terms of the notion of importance. The work of the caring professions is said to be more important than that of many others and so must be rewarded accordingly; and within the professions the work of some people is more important than that of others. But this notion of importance is really part of a wider notion of quality or merit, to which we now turn.

The most common, and the most philosophically intractable, idea advanced to defend differentials in pay is in terms of the quality of the work. We shall discuss this issue for simplicity in terms of the health professions. Let us start with the idea that medical workers ought to get more pay in so far as they are especially *skilled*. Now presumably the idea is not just that ability as such ought to be rewarded. We do not think that it would be just to give everyone an IQ test and reward the highest scores, if only because IQs are supposed to be something for which the possessor can claim no credit. Rather the idea is that *acquired* skills should be rewarded. This idea can be explained in terms of compensation. It is undoubtedly a burden to acquire the skills in question (though even a medical student's life is not without its pleasures), and students also lose financially in that they give up the wages they could be earning during their student years. There is no philosophical problem about the claim that doctors and other skilled medical workers deserve some extra money for these reasons, and there is also of course the utilitarian argument that without such compensations not enough people will take on these jobs. (It should be noted that both these compensation arguments, from desert and from utility, apply in varying degrees to many skilled occupations.)

The other argument which comes under this heading of 'quality' concerns the value of the work to society. Caring workers, it is said, are of absolutely vital importance and their pay must reflect this. But this claim needs further investigation. After all, sewage workers and dustmen are of vital importance to society and no one suggests they should be paid on the same level as doctors or social workers. Part of the difference is that caring workers, especially medical workers, are concerned with what is urgent, with rectifying disasters, so their work seems especially important. But this quality of urgency applies also to the work of firemen and to policemen. Perhaps then what is claimed is that those with jobs which deal with crises should be highly paid (with further compensating differentials to account for different degrees of skill). But then it is not clear why those dealing with crises *deserve* more than others, apart from due allowances for extra skill, and for danger where applicable. After all, everyone cannot be a crisis worker. They are dependent on the rest of the community for their work, just as we are dependent on them for their help. What is clear, however, is that crisis workers, because of the urgent nature of their work, have an enormous power of *blackmail*, and the more skilled they are the more that is the case, because they are harder to replace. In this purely market sense they are very valuable, and so it may be useful to pay them more than considerations based on their skill alone would warrant, if this is necessary in order to have enough of them.

The final argument we shall consider is the straight comparison: 'In Sweden/USA/West Germany they pay their doctors/nurses/social workers much better.' What kind of argument is this? It may be a piece of evidence as to possibilities – 'they find the money somehow, so it can be done' – but of course it does not amount to much unless all the differences in circumstance between one country and another are allowed for. It may be an appeal to authority, the tacit assumption being that if country X does it, it must be right. But then this assumption can always be challenged. It may be a move in the blackmail mentioned in the previous paragraph, a way of saying, 'If you don't pay us more, we'll go to America.' This threat, if meant, might provide a utilitarian argument for paying more. Finally, this argument, or move in an argument, is sometimes what one might call a request for a reward for altruism: in effect, what is being said is, 'All right, we don't think it right to decamp to the USA, but it's unfair that we should do quite so badly out of doing the right thing.' This is endearing, but no one has a right not to suffer from doing what he thinks is right.

Finally let us suppose that, as a result of considering and weighing up all the factors we have been discussing, a caring worker comes to the conclusion that he deserves more money. What steps may he take to get it? People sometimes assume that if a person's claim is just, it follows that anything he does to press it is in itself justified, though they would normally allow that he may have overriding obligations not to press the claim in certain ways. Indeed, this assumption can seem a logical truth – if he has a right to get something, surely he has a right to adopt the means of getting it. But this is a confusion between rights of action and rights of recipience. If a person has a right to a certain salary, this is a right of recipience, a right to be given something by someone else whose duty it is to give it. But a right to *do* something – strike, say – is a right of action, an absence of obligation to refrain. No particular rights of action follow logically from a right of recipience. It may be that someone denied his rights always has some rights of action. But then it is a matter not of logic but of moral judgment what these are. It is difficult to see, for example, how they could be held to include inflicting suffering of greater magnitude than the lost right involves on those who have no duty at all in the matter and so are not at fault.

4 The knowledge base
of the
caring professions

Medicine and the natural sciences

In this chapter we shall be concerned with the sort of knowledge
on which medicine and social work are based. At first sight it
seems obviously correct to say that medicine is based on the
natural sciences and social work on the social sciences. We shall
later argue that this claim is greatly oversimplified and shall
suggest fundamental ways in which it ought to be modified, but
there is a lot to be said for assuming the distinction as a working
hypothesis. We shall therefore begin by examining the nature of
the natural sciences on which medicine is thought to be founded.

Historically speaking there can be few natural sciences which
have not been thought relevant to medicine. Apart from the
biological sciences, which have always been thought to be
relevant, medical practitioners looked to astronomy in ancient
times for assistance, and now turn in a variety of ways to
mathematics, physics and computing. It would seem, then, that
there is no one type of science which is uniquely relevant to
medicine, and indeed what is called 'medical science' is just a convenient label for a group of sciences studied by medical students;
what is in the group will vary to some extent from one historical
period to the next. It might therefore be helpful to enquire
whether there are any characteristics shared by all the sciences. Is

there something we could call 'the scientific approach to the world' which would be the real basis of medicine, and, in so far as the social sciences are genuine sciences, of social work as well?

One fruitful answer to this question is that all sciences, whether physical, biological or social, are concerned with the search for patterns or uniformities in their subject-matters. Obviously, orders of many varieties can be traced in nature, from the microscopic to the macroscopic, or, from another point of view, we could say that nature can be ordered in different ways according to the purposes of the scientists. Let us look at examples of these orders.

There is one type of order so familiar that it generally escapes notice. All of us recognize *things* – a table, a rose, a bit of iron – and we assign those names in virtue of an ordered conjunction of properties which we wish to distinguish from other ordered conjunctions of properties. Some of these orders seem to be discovered in nature, as a tree or a mountain, and others seem to be human artefacts, as a knife or a pair of trousers, but in fact whatever we regard as a 'thing' depends to some extent on human needs and interests. For this reason the classification of 'things' in nature is never complete since human interests change and develop, and we develop our language to enable us to make new discriminations.

Yet although from this point of view the identification of 'things' in nature is inevitably anthropocentric, from another point of view 'things' have characteristics which do not depend on human perceptions. First of all, a 'thing' must have a certain *temporal duration*, it must last 'long enough' – a lightning flash does not satisfy this criterion and could not be regarded as a thing. Second, the duration of a thing must be *continuous* – there must be no gaps in its existence., Third, any qualitative changes in a thing must themselves be regular or follow patterns. For example, if we heat a piece of wax the changes in colour, smell, consistency, etc., follow regular patterns.[1]

The concept of a 'thing' is fundamental to our world as ordinary agents. To say this is not to say that non-things, such as sounds, tastes, smells, flashes of light and so on are unimportant to human life – on the contrary, they are of profound importance for our grasp and enjoyment of the world – but it is to say that we could not identify these or recognize them if we did not first have the concept of a thing. In this sense, a thing has a logical or meta-physical priority.[2]

The logical or metaphysical priority of the thing emerges also when we move on to look at the types of order or uniformity with which natural history or elementary science is concerned. The most basic of these types of uniformity is that involving the uniform association of attributes, such as 'Iron rusts in damp conditions' or 'Common salt is soluble in water'. The perception of uniformities of this sort is important for the classification of things into kinds. For instance, chemical substances can be dis-tinguished by us because we find that certain attributes of matter uniformly carry with them certain other attributes, and biological species can be distinguished because we find that there are uniform associations of attributes in living organisms. The perception of uniformities of this sort is really just a systematic extension of the discrimination of the world into things of which we have been speaking. Thus, there is no sharp line between our common-sense knowledge of the world in terms of its 'things' and scientific knowledge, in that the basis on which the scientist begins his investigations is the series of classifications we call 'natural history', and natural history is simply the drawing attention in a systematic way to the properties possessed by types of thing.

Moving from the classifications of natural history to the types of order or uniformity with which scientists are more characteris-tically concerned, we find scientific laws dealing with the *uniformities of change or development* to be found in natural processes.[3] Laws of this kind are common in medical science: they might state the stages, say, in the development of an embryo, or the course of a disease. For example, it is a law of the develop-ment of an embryo that the formation of the lungs never precedes the formation of the circulatory system.

Another type of law deals with *numerical constants in nature*. Into this group fall laws concerned with the melting points of chemical substances or the propagation of sound or light. Yet another type of law deals with *functional relationships* between measurable quantities, such as the law that for any gas $PV = KT$ (where P stands for pressure, V for volume, T for absolute temperature, while K is a constant depending only on the units of measurement chosen). The functional relationship need not be simple but may be of any type recognized in mathematics, provided only that for each value of a certain variable or variables there should be only one value of another variable.

Quantitative laws of the last two types have been formulated only in the more recent stages of scientific development, and sometimes they can be regarded as refinements of previously known qualitative laws. For example, it was known in prehistoric times that iron melted at a great heat, and a quantitative law expressing on a scale of temperature precisely at what point iron melts can be regarded as a more precise formulation of this early perception. Again, it was known from early times that a projectile follows a curved path, but Galileo was able to show that the path is a semi-parabola. More recently some quantitative laws have been expressed *statistically*. Laws of this kind are to be found in physics, in biology and especially in the social sciences.

The importance of quantitative precision in science is so great that some scientists argue that no law is properly scientific unless it is purely quantitative. The arguments behind this view are: that true science must be precise, and only the quantitative is precise; and that true science must be beyond the subjective, the realm of personal opinions and interpretations, and only the quantitative takes us beyond this realm. These arguments are not convincing. First, laws such as the developmental ones earlier mentioned do not seem to be open to quantitative formulation, but they are still precise. Second, even quantitative laws are concerned in the end with *things* of certain kinds and so they can never be assimilated entirely to purely mathematical formulae. Third, some laws, such as the statistical ones we mentioned, are quantitative but cannot be absolutely precise since they express only relative frequencies. Fourth, even the quantitative can be open to different interpretations, as is notorious in the case of statistical findings; it is naive to think that only the qualitative is controversial.

To sum up so far, we have been arguing that our understanding of the world is necessarily based on the concept of the thing. On the basis of this metaphysical unit science extends our understanding of nature, first through the classifications of natural history, and then through developmental laws to numerical laws of various kinds, such as those concerned with numerical constants, with functional relationships and with statistical frequencies. It is doubtful, however, whether it is helpful to restrict the term 'scientific' to quantitative laws; certainly, the quantitative can still be the controversial.

So far we have been characterizing the scientific approach to nature in terms of an *aim* – the search for order. But science can also be characterized in terms of its use of a certain *method* – the experimental method. Just as the scientific search for uniformity in nature is an extension of our everyday perception of uniformity in our surroundings, so the scientific use of observation and experiment can be seen as an extension of our everyday observation of what happens. And just as there is no one type of uniformity in nature, so there is no one aim of experiment in science.

First of all, experiments or systematic investigations may be used *to test 'accepted facts'*. For example, Boyle, in *The Sceptical Chymist*, describes how he tested such doctrines of the ancients as the theory of the four elements in nature and found them wanting.[4] Similarly, in medicine it may be held that there is a correlation between certain sorts of coronary or respiratory diseases and certain sorts of urban environments. Precise investigation of this might show that the urban environment is less important than the chemical composition of the water supply. Studies of this kind are prominent in social science when sociologists or psychologists might question 'accepted facts'. For example, it used to be believed that when children were in hospital parental visiting was unsettling for them, on the evidence that children cried when their parents left. More detailed investigation of this phenomenon, however, has suggested that the appearance is misleading, and that children are less likely to be damaged by a stay in hospital if parents can visit frequently.

Second, experiments may be devised *to check random observations*. Sometimes in the course of his work a scientist may notice something unusual and wish to reproduce this, in order to examine its significance. More commonly, third, experiments may be used *to find out what is the case*. These are exploratory experiments. It would be unusual however for experiments to be purely random and exploratory. More commonly a scientist will have some embryonic ideas about what he is looking for, even if he lacks a full-scale hypothesis. Fruitful experiments, in other words, tend to be for or against some general hypothesis.

This takes us, fourth, to the use of experiment *to test hypotheses*.

For example Galileo, using a geometrical method, reached the hypothesis that the spaces described by a body falling from a state of rest with a uniformly accelerated motion are to each other as the squares of the time intervals employed in traversing these distances ($S = \frac{1}{2} at^2$). Having formulated his hypothesis Galileo proceeded to test it by an experiment with balls rolling down an inclined plane.

It should be noted, however, that whereas experiments can disconfirm a hypothesis they cannot conclusively establish it. Thus, a scientist may know that if hypothesis H is valid then consequences *p q r* must follow. He may be able to devise experiments to check whether these consequences do follow. If they do not follow then H can be rejected. But if *p q r* do follow, then, whereas they render H more *probable*, they do not logically establish it, because it could well be that H2 could equally explain the occurrence of *p q r*. Moreover, even if experiments *disconfirm* a hypothesis the disproof is logically conclusive only against a background of assumptions which are not themselves questioned in the experiments. Thus the logic of hypothesis testing may be set out as follows. Let us call the assumptions K. If H(K) then p q r ... But p q r are not confirmed; then either H is false or K is false or both are false. If H(K) then p q r ... But experiments confirm p q r; then H(K) is probable, although H2K may also be probable.

Three conclusions emerge from this. The first is the tentative nature of scientific findings, always open to revision in whole or in part; the second is the close connection between theory and experiment in science; the third is the importance of the general assumptions (K) for the whole enterprise of science.

What is the nature of the knowledge which the natural sciences give us of the world? In view of what we have just said it would seem that they can provide only tentative generalizations about the world – what seem to be constant conjunctions of events. Yet the natural sciences often seem to be going beyond the statement of tentative empirical generalizations about uniformities in nature; they seem rather to be telling us what must of *necessity* happen, and they are often so regarded by scientists.

There are several reasons for these apparently discrepant views about the nature of science. The first is a confusion between the status of a scientific law, on the one hand, and the status of an assertion of the *relationship* between such a law and an inference drawn from it, on the other. Thus, if a scientist has correctly identified a situation, and has correctly decided what laws are relevant to it, then his laws will tell him what he may expect to happen in the situation, with the tacit proviso that all the conditions are fulfilled for the correct application of the relevant laws. In this case, his prediction, since it is based on an empirical generalization, may turn out to be false. But if we frame a proposition of the following form – 'If all ice melts at 0°C, and if this is a piece of ice, then it will melt at 0°C' – then we are asserting a truth of logic which logically cannot be falsified by anything which happens. Here we can legitimately speak of what must of necessity happen.

A second reason for the apparent discrepancy is the failure to note, on the one hand, the variety of laws there are, and, on the other, the function which certain high-level laws or principles have in a theory. Thus, to take the first point, there is clearly a difference in logical status between an empirical generalization like Fechner's Law – the eye can distinguish differences in illumination which are a constant (approximately 0.01) fraction of the total illumination – and the Second Law of Thermodynamics; one could easily be abandoned without serious damage to science whereas the second is absolutely fundamental. The point, however, is not that nature necessarily operates in terms of the Second Law of Thermodynamics, but that physicists choose to understand the physical world in terms of it in that they will not permit contrary evidence to count against it. The necessity of high-level laws reflects the tenacity with which scientists hold on to these laws and principles. Yet even the most tenaciously-held principle is in the end abandoned when the evidence against it is so great that it becomes simpler to abandon it than to explain away the evidence. Even the geocentric view of the world was finally abandoned.

If this analysis has been on the right lines we are left with the picture of a hierarchy of scientific laws. At one end there are empirical generalizations, describing observable uniformities, which can be overthrown by contrary instances without disturbing the total framework. At the other end there are principles or 'laws of nature' which are basic to the organization of scientific theory and which scientists are reluctant to abandon. It is largely a matter of scientific convenience, or other contingency, at what point in the hierarchy a uniform pattern is termed a scientific law, and at what point a scientific law becomes 'a law of nature'. Thus science both *discovers* uniformities and *imposes* uniformities; it not only helps us to understand the world by telling us what is there in the world, it helps us to understand by creating frameworks through which we must, for a given historical period, view the world.

What are the fundamental assumptions underlying this approach to the world? As we have seen, one assumption is that of the existence of *things*; we cannot understand the world without making use of this basic category. A second fundamental assumption emerges if we consider again that the scientist searches for patterns or uniformities in the events to which things give rise. For to 'give rise' to an event in this sense is to *cause* it to happen, and to search for uniformities in these events is to search for causal laws. It is true that scientists have sometimes said that they are not seeking causes but are simply trying to describe regularities in nature. Galileo and Newton, for example, explicitly put aside the idea that they were searching for the causes of motion; rather, they regarded themselves as describing quantitatively different types of motion.[5] Nevertheless, this search for uniformity would make no sense unless the scientist were presupposing, at the least, that the future would resemble the past, and to presuppose this is to presuppose that there are underlying causes. Indeed, the assumption of causality is so fundamental to our understanding of the world that, like the concept of the thing, it is part of the structure of our ordinary outlook on the world. To put it another way, it is part of our conception of a thing; to be a thing is to act and react in a predictable, law-like manner, or to be governed by causality. We shall later put forward factors which suggest that the assumption of causality is not necessary for an activity to be called scientific, but these factors, even if genuine, do not suggest that the principle of causality is not an essential part of our ordinary spectator outlook on the world.

A science of human beings

Do the social sciences provide a science or sciences of human beings analogous to the sciences of disease on which medicine is based? This question clearly concerns the nature of the knowledge on which social work is based, but it is relevant to medicine as well as to social work, because, while it is true that medicine is based on the natural sciences, it is by no means the whole truth about medical practice. Physicians and surgeons, dentists, nurses and most members of the medical profession are not simply medical scientists – they are dealing with patients. In other words, whereas it is a commonplace of modern medicine that it is scientific, it is also a commonplace that the medical profession treats patients and not just diseases. The question of the possibility of a science of human beings and their actions is therefore as relevant to medical as to social work practice. Can there be such a science?

If there is the possibility of such a science then it is reasonable to expect that it will have characteristics similar to those found in the sciences of nature. Now the natural scientist, we said, searches for uniformities in the events of the world, and expresses the uniformities in terms of laws of various sorts, and we argued that this kind of search would make no sense unless scientists assumed that the uniformities are *causally determined*. Indeed, it was our earlier contention that the scientific search for uniformity is an extension of the tendency of us all to comprehend our world in terms of our identification of *things* and their properties, and our conception of a 'thing' necessarily includes the belief that it is causally determined. We can therefore say that the assumption of causal determinism in nature is a necessary part of the attitude we all have towards the world and its events. Now if there is a social science of human beings analogous to natural science it is plausible to maintain that the data of social science – human actions – must be subject to laws in a manner similar to that in which events in the natural world are law-like. In short, human actions must be causally determined. This is a persuasive thesis because it can be regarded as a logical implication of the general thesis of determinism in nature: since every event in nature seems to be determined, at least as far as the macroscopic world is concerned, it would seem to be rational to hold that human actions, in so far as they are events, must also be determined. Moreover, if determinism is not applicable to human actions then we are left with an order of events which is beyond the reach of complete scientific explanation and is therefore logically odd. Now, although these seem good reasons for accepting an extension of the programme of determinism to human action, there are implications for our ordinary views of ourselves and our actions which must be faced. To bring these out let us look first at the nature of human action.

We talk about our own actions essentially in terms of purpose. Thus, we say, 'I did X because I wanted Y', or 'He did X in order to get Y'. Now there are three features of such accounts of action in terms of purpose. The first and most obvious feature is that they make an essential reference to a *desire* or *want*; to describe human purposiveness is essentially to describe human desires and wants. The second and less obvious feature is that they essentially presuppose a *choice* or *decision* to let the desire for the end carry us into action. This is brought out by the fact that to an explanation of the form 'I did X because I wanted Y' it is always possible to add 'and I *chose* to act on my desire'. Moreover, this addition is required for logical completeness (although, of course, it is often considered redundant within the context of ordinary conversation). For people very often have desires on which they do not act. Thus, in a detective story several people may have motives for the crime, that is, they have aims in terms of which the committing of the crime may be explained; but only one of the suspects acts on his desire. There is therefore a gap between desire and action, and it is possible to say that the concept of choice or decision fills it. The third feature is that accounts of action in terms of purpose imply that the agent is morally responsible for his actions in so far as his actions issue from his will as an expression of his desires.

If this is a fair description of the nature of action – its essential features – there are good reasons for maintaining that it is not compatible with the programme of determinism as that applies to human actions. The first reason is that if a cause is regarded as 'that which makes an event happen' a caused action cannot also be regarded as 'freely chosen'. But free choice was one of the essential features of characteristically human purposiveness. The second reason is that that which is not 'freely chosen' does not seem to be our action, an expression of our will, and if it is not, then our belief in moral responsibility will require radical revision. But our belief in moral responsibility is one of our most deeply rooted.

Some proponents of the thesis of determinism are not concerned by the fact that it may seem to cast doubt on fundamental convictions about ourselves and our actions, such as the three we have just mentioned. Other philosophers, however, hold no less firmly to the belief that our conviction of moral responsibility, say, is as rationally founded as our conviction that every event has a cause. For them there are two possibilities: either to try to *reconcile* the beliefs we have as agents with the thesis of determinism, or more drastically to reject the thesis of determinism as that applies to human action. Let us look at the first of these possibilities, and state it in terms of physical determinism, as represented by the medical science of neurology. The physical determinist can concede that the use of purposive language in our ordinary explanations of action is entirely legitimate, but he goes on to argue that those processes which were said to be essential to purposive behaviour, such as 'making a choice', 'taking a decision', 'carrying out an intention' and so on, have physical counterparts in the brain and that he can provide a sufficient causal explanation of these physical counterparts in terms of the science of neurology. It should be noted, however, that if the physical determinist is going to give 'teeth' to his thesis he must be precise in his interpretation of 'physical counterpart'. It can be agreed by all that decisions have physical correlates in the sense that unless certain physical conditions obtain – the person's brain is in good working order, various nervous impulses occur, etc., – a decision cannot in fact be made. To admit this is simply to admit that the occurrence of physical events is a necessary condition of the making of a decision. The physical determinist, however, must as a determinist say more than this. He must maintain that decisions and the like have physical *determinants* in the brain, that the occurrence of physical events is both a necessary and a sufficient condition of the occurrence (for 'occurrence' it would really be) of a decision.

The thesis of the physical determinist can be made more dramatically compelling if it is expressed in terms of an analogy between the human brain and nervous system and a computer. The arguments of the physical determinist are apt to seem unconvincing if they seem to be saying that the human brain is just a machine; for whereas the conception of a machine stimulated the imagination of writers in the seventeenth and early eighteenth centuries it now seems hopelessly inadequate as an analogy to explain the workings of the human brain. The conception of the computer, however, is to the imagination of the twentieth century what that of the machine was to earlier centuries – a model which, in its close parallels with the workings of the brain, helps us to understand what is otherwise mysterious. A computer, it can be argued, is a physically determined system: it is an input/output mechanism in which every event can be causally connected with sets of preceding events. And so it is with the brain.

The question now arises as to the relationship between physical determinism and our ordinary agent-conceptions of action and responsibility. It might be maintained that the two are compatible, in that while physical determinism provides an explanation of the occurrence of *events*, no explanation of events can logically amount to an explanation of *actions* because events and actions belong to different and irreducible categories. In other words, physical determinism is a theory about events, in the brain and elsewhere, but no theory of events can ever be adequate as a theory of action. For example, let us take an action such as posting a letter. The claim is that an action-description of the form 'posting a letter' involves the use of concepts which are irreducibly social in nature and logically cannot be reduced to, or analysed in terms of, the colourless scientific language of event-descriptions. Both languages are necessary for our understanding of the world, but the language of action-descriptions can never be replaced by the language of event-descriptions.

To bring out the truth in this argument let us take the example of a puppeteer whose puppets are acting a play from a foreign culture. A commentator is describing and explaining the actions and their significance to the audience. Now it is true that the commentator's description of the actions cannot, logically cannot, be replaced by a description of the jerkings of the wires. These are complementary languages which must continue to exist side by side. This is the element of truth in the 'compatibility' argument. But the example also serves to bring out the fact that the commentator's descriptions, while they cannot exactly be replaced by, are nevertheless undercut by, or are parasitic on, the jerkings of the wires. The purposive behaviour attributed to the puppets is explained at a deeper level by physical causality. The puppets have no choice, and the purposes attributed to them are fantasy.

Now if the physical determinist is correct then we are in the same predicament as the puppets, and the purposes we entertain and attribute to others are no more real than those attributed to the puppets by the commentator. It seems then that we must either regard physical determinism as inapplicable to human action or regard our ordinary conceptions of action as illusory. For action essentially involves purposiveness and purposiveness seems to involve, not simply choice, but an undetermined choice – a choice which could have been different in exactly the same situation. For, if purposiveness is to be the criterion of responsible action, it must be taken to allow that the agent could have done otherwise than he did. This seems to be demanded by the notion that it is *his* action, that he is responsible for it, in the sense of making it what it is.

There is an objection of a different sort to the idea of a science of human action based on physical determinism. So far we have objected that if such a science is valid then our ordinary conceptions of action, purpose and responsibility must be based on an illusion, but it is also possible to object that if such a science is valid then the idea of a deterministic *social science* must also be based on an illusion. The reason is that social scientists, while they may point out that the conception of purposive action is problematic and complex, and that our ordinary assumptions and ways of regarding purpose do not do justice to these complexities, nevertheless essentially retain the category of the purposive as irreducible and indispensable for the scientific explanation of human action. In other words, if, as the physical determinist is committed to holding, our ordinary beliefs about ourselves are illusory, then a social science assuming these ordinary beliefs as its basic data must also be illusory.

If it is therefore the case that the social sciences do retain the concept of purpose (however complexly understood) as indispensable for the understanding of human action, how, if at all, is a deterministic social science of human action possible? It might be possible, if we were able to give a causal account of purposive action at the psychological rather than the neurological level. Let us examine this possibility of a deterministic social science of psychology.

Human beings and psychological determinism

The psychological determinist agrees that we may legitimately use purposive language in explaining actions and that we rightly assume ourselves to be morally responsible for our actions. He also agrees that actions are events and as such are open to sufficient explanation in causal terms. His solution of this apparent antinomy is to suggest, first, that it is at best misleading to say that the causes of human action compel (since they are the agent's own choices), and in any case it may be false to regard *any* causes as compelling events to happen; second, that purposive types of explanation (including the 'choice' requirement) are all reducible to explanations in terms of desire; and third, that desires are causes (but only in the non-coercive, 'innocent' manner to be made clear in the development of the first step). The aim of this argument is to reduce purposive explanation to causal and so preserve both the agent's assumption of moral responsibility and the spectator's assumption of causation. Let us look in more detail at the steps in this argument.

The first step was to point out that that which gives rise to action is the agent's own choice, and it is misleading to regard this as something which 'compels' an action to happen. 'Compulsion', it may be said, simply means 'absence of choice'. Hence, if the psychological determinist is correct in interpreting choice as a cause it is not fair to say he is suggesting that we are acting under compulsion. Moreover, the psychological determinist usually endorses the empiricist analysis of causation. If so, he will deny that it is meaningful to speak in general of causes as 'compelling'. On the empiricist analysis, causal laws simply record regular conjunctions of events, what in fact happens in nature, and do not require us to speak of compulsion. This analysis of causation – which we shall concede for the sake of argument – certainly seems to remove the apparent implication of determinism that our actions are 'compelled' by alien forces. The claim is that the causes of our actions are our own desires, and we are therefore not compelled from outside ourselves. Let us accept the first step.

The second step was to assert that purposive explanations are all reducible to explanations in terms of the agent's desires. While it is true that we have already defined purposive statements (verbally at least) as those which can be cast in the form 'I did A because I wanted B', we also stressed that the desire for the end presupposed in purposive explanations is never a sufficient condition of action, for it is always possible (and required for logical completeness) to add 'and I chose to act on my desire for B'. It follows, then, that if the psychological determinist is to make out a case for reducing purposive explanations to causal he must be able to reduce choice to desire. The case is characteristically made out by the drawing of a distinction between the mere occurrence of 'blind' desire and the modification such desire may receive after the agent has deliberated about the consequences of acting upon it and other desires he may have. Desire need not be either 'blind' or 'compulsive'; although each single desire may be concentrated on a single feature of an imagined future, it is possible to deliberate about the consequences of following one desire or another and thus strengthen some desires and weaken others. For the psychological determinist choice is the result of this reflective survey of our desires and their believed consequences; it is simply 'processed' desire.

Does this deterministic analysis of choice provide an adequate account of purposive action? In particular, does it seem adequate to the idea that our actions are in some ineradicable way *ours*, an expression of our will? There are two apparent difficulties here. The first concerns the situation in which our desires are focused on the attainment of a specific goal X, but we know that we *ought* to do Y. With a struggle we choose Y against our desires. In this situation it is Y rather than X which is the expression of our will, and in this situation Y is *chosen* and the choice is not analyzable in terms of our desires which are *ex hypothesi* concentrated on X. It might be objected here that our own analysis of purposive action stipulated that in all cases a desire for an end is presupposed. Hence, there must be a desire for Y. This is true, but it need not be the *strongest* desire, and in this case we are arguing that our strongest desire is for X, but that we do Y because we (weakly) desire to do it (perhaps because it is our duty) and *choose* to act on this desire. It might be further objected that our strongest desire *must* be for Y because that is what we in fact do, but if this necessity is simply assumed, then the claim that we always act on our strongest desire has been made true by definition, and nothing of substance follows from a stipulated definition.

The second difficulty concerns the difference between our knowledge of causes and our knowledge of our own will. Knowledge of causes is inductive, based on experience or evidence: knowledge of choice is non-inductive, non-experiential, non-evidential. If a person claims to know that A is B we can always ask him how he knows, and the appropriate response will be in terms of evidence. But if someone states he has chosen to X and we ask him how he knows, the appropriate response is a baffled stare, for the question does not make sense! It does not make sense because our knowledge of our own decisions is immediate and incorrigible. To attempt to analyse choice in terms of causality is to attempt to sever it from our will and connect it with the processes of natural events. This does violence to our ordinary conceptions of action, and *a fortiori* it would do violence to our convictions of moral responsibility.

The explanation of action

We suggest, then, that those explanations of action which betoken responsibility, such as 'I did it because I wanted...', imply also 'I did it because I chose to do it' – construing choice not in a deterministic sense but in the sense which embodies the notion that in a particular set of circumstances a choice may go one way or the other. In other words, we maintain that responsibility entails the 'categorical substitutability' of choices, i.e. the possibility that the choice might be different, not merely *if* the circumstances were also different, but different in the same circumstances. We can also say that responsibility entails the categorical substitutability of *actions*. This is not really a separate factor from the categorical substitutability of choices. Rather our view is that responsible action is action which embodies a choice of an undetermined kind; and to describe this situation we can speak indifferently of the categorical substitutability of actions or of the categorical substitutability of choices.

It might of course be said that in that case 'I did it because I chose to' does not add anything to an explanation. After all, it does not necessarily even explain an action in terms of an antecedent, since choice of this kind need not precede the action but may be manifested in the actual performing of it. But the force of the explanation lies not in what it says but in what it

excludes. For if such an explanation implies that the circumstances might all have been exactly the same but the choice or
chosen action different, it rules out a causal explanation of the
same action: in causal terms, only one effect can follow a given set
of circumstances. We might strengthen our position by pointing
out that if an action can be causally explained, it is fixed long
before the person concerned is born (indeed, from the beginnings
of the universe); and an action thus determined would not be the
agent's action at all, for what happens depends in the end on
factors completely beyond his control. The chosen action, on the
other hand, is the agent's own doing; he may be circumscribed by
features which he cannot influence, including his own desires,
but some room is left for his own decision to contribute to events.
The consequence is that we cannot reconcile the standpoints of
the agent and the scientific observer of events and we must
conclude that, if we are to hold on to our ordinary concepts of
action, we must deny that actions are always open to sufficient
explanation in causal terms.

How then are we to explain why people perform those actions
which they do perform? Let us suppose that a person says, 'I did
A because I chose to do it.' Clearly this does not amount to an
explanation so much as a *claim*: 'I am responsible for this action'
or 'This action is mine'. If such a claim is made we can go on to
ask, 'Why did you choose to do it?' To this question a typical
answer would be 'because I wanted such-and-such', and this reply
seems to explain the action in a way in which the bare mention of
choice does not – it is informative. Our discussion therefore
seems to show that purposive explanation has two components: a
choice component which (as we have seen) serves merely
negatively to exclude causal explanation, and a desire component
which provides positive information.

But what kind of information does such explanation provide?
To raise this question is to begin discussion of the third step in
the psychological determinist's argument, when he maintained
that desire is a cause. It is certainly true that our desires are
causally conditioned, that there are explanations in psychological, sociological and indeed biochemical terms as to why
certain desires occur in certain people at certain times. But to
concede that our desires are causally conditioned is not to
concede that desires cause actions, in the strong sense that the

occurrence of a desire is a sufficient condition for the performance of an action. Indeed, some philosophers would argue that
desires logically cannot be causes because they are not in the
appropriate logical category to be causes. For example, it is
arguable that desires are *dispositions* to act in certain ways,
whereas causes must be *events*. We need not take sides in this
controversy, however, for our contention is not that desires
logically cannot be causes, but only that they logically cannot be
the *sufficient conditions* of action. In other words, we insist that
there is an essential place in action for *choice*, and choice is a non-
causal condition of action. There are therefore in our scheme two
independently necessary conditions of action, and whether the
'desire' condition is regarded as causal or not is not a central
issue. More important than the question of whether the 'desire'
component is causal or not is the question of what its function is
as an explanation of action. Let us briefly suggest an answer to
this question.

To mention a desire is to show the *point* of a choice or to make
sense of it. For example, if we ask why a man decided to tidy his
garden and are told that he wants to sell his house, we see the
point of his decision. The explanation sets the chosen action in a
framework: sometimes, as here, a framework of familiar human
purposes; sometimes a framework which may itself require
illumination by reference to a further want. And this is the kind
of explanation which we are ordinarily looking for when we ask
why someone does something. We maintain, then, that the only
informative explanation of responsible action is of the 'because he
wanted' type, to be construed as giving the sense or point of an
action, where 'sense' or 'point' may be understood as referring to
necessary but not sufficient conditions.

Social science and action

What are the implications of this analysis of human action, with
its resistance to determinism, for a social science of human
action? If, as we have maintained, science is the search for uniformities and patterns in our experience, then we have by no means
ruled out the possibility of a social science. We have ruled out
only the possibility that the patterns in human action have
sufficient causal conditions. The task for social science can

therefore be seen as the tracing of the patterns or systems of influences which shape human purposes. Some of these patterns are economic, some political, some legal, some religious or ideological, and so on. Knowledge of these frameworks is of great assistance in understanding human behaviour.

In tracing the patterns into which human behaviour tends to fall social scientists frequently use the term 'social role'. While there is no unambiguous use of the concept, far less a definition of it, it is a useful tool of social science in that it can act as a bridge concept to explain the influence of society on the conduct of the individual.[6] Thus, individuals act in society *as* labourers, builders, musicians, farmers, teachers, doctors, probation officers, fathers, etc. where these terms indicate a social function. But while individuals act in these roles, thus contributing to the maintenance of society, the roles in turn shape and influence the whole personality of the persons who act in them. For this reason, a knowledge of the social sciences is essential for any adequate understanding of individual action, because the influence of society is present in every individual action. This point, which has for long been recognized in the education of the social worker, is gradually being appreciated by the medical profession. Thus, it is coming to be accepted that not only do social influences affect the course and incidence of disease, but that the very *definition* of disease is at least as much a social as a physical matter. A knowledge of the social sciences would therefore be of great assistance to a medical practitioner.

An undue emphasis on one social science can of course distort our view of human behaviour. For example, it is accepted in social science that economic influences are exceedingly important in shaping human behaviour, whether that of individuals, groups or nations. But 'rational economic man' is an abstraction and does not correspond to any one actual person (see p.102). People do not often, if ever, act from purely economic motives, or at least it is a simplistic assumption that they *always* do; someone may well sacrifice an economic gain for reasons of social status, love, spitefulness, or high moral principle. Of course, a doctrinaire social scientist might reply that all these apparently diverse motives can alike be classified as 'preferences' and measured economically, but this move encourages us to see uniformity in human motivation where there is in fact complexity. People certainly act in social roles, but not just in one; and the difficulty in applying social science to human behaviour is that of knowing the relevance of the different frames of reference of the different social sciences. Nothing brings the social sciences into greater disrepute than the pretensions of one social scientist – a Freudian psychologist, or a Marxian economist, say – to explain *all* human behaviour in terms of a few simplistic concepts. This can be said without at all decrying the great explanatory power of both Freudian psychology and Marxian economics. We suggest, then, that while a knowledge of the different patterns elaborated in the social sciences is a help in understanding human behaviour, these patterns are abstractions from the complex reality of individual human conduct, and since the doctor, nurse, dentist and social worker are concerned with *this* individual, or *this* family group or *this* neighbourhood, there are limits to the explanatory power of social science and dangers of distortion in uncritical use of scientific frames of reference.

We wish, further, to suggest *radical* limitations to the explanatory power of the social sciences as they apply to human behaviour. To bring these out let us consider the connection between being a person and having a role. It might first be suggested that the relationship is one of identity, in the sense that acting as a person just is acting *as* an X, Y or Z, where these name a social role. If this thesis were valid, then, subject to the difficulties we have mentioned of knowing which explanatory frameworks to apply, it would be possible to have a complete explanation of human behaviour in terms of one or more social sciences. For there can be detailed objective descriptions of the roles which people play.

This account, however, omits to mention one essential aspect of every action – the choice requirement. People can choose to accept or reject their roles. Moreover, while playing the role of doctor, social worker, teacher, nurse, father, trade unionist, etc., a person can be *detached* from his roles, can laugh at himself in them. This suggests that there is an important *personal* dimension to action which is not caught by the concept of a social role. In other words, to understand an action it is important to know how the person himself sees the action, or more generally what is his attitude to his role. And understanding of this kind does not come from applying any social science to action.

At this point three different objections may be levelled at the thesis that there is an irreducibly personal element in any action which cannot be explained in terms of any one or more social sciences. The first is that all human actions must be understood in terms of the patterns which make up social roles, because all actions are social in nature. In discussing this objection we could consider the meaning of the premise that 'All actions are social in nature'. If I am working alone in my house and make myself a cup of coffee it is not immediately obvious in what sense my actions are social since no one is there to witness or participate in them. The reply might be that the action 'making a cup of coffee' can be understood only as part of a whole way of life, or even that I could not make a cup of coffee unless the ingredients, fuel-supply, etc., were provided by other members of society. This may well be true, but it is now only in a trivial sense that 'All actions are social in nature'. Fortunately, however, we need not enter into a discussion of this, because our thesis is that all actions have an irreducible personal dimension, and that thesis is consistent with the claim that all actions are social in nature in the minimal sense that they require at least some social concepts for their complete description.

The second objection is that 'person' is itself a role-concept, and that therefore what we are calling the 'personal' dimension to action can still be explained in terms of the social sciences which deal with the concept of a role. Now there is a great deal to be said for the view that 'person' is a role-concept. Consider, for example, the history of the term 'person'. Historians of ideas tell us that the term 'person' is derived from the Latin *persona*, which was originally a mask through which came the sound of an actor's voice. The term is then extended to mean a role in the drama or *dramatis persona*, and from there it easily comes to mean a social role. It is in this sense that the term *persona* is used in Roman law, where it stands for someone as a subject of rights. In other words, the history of the word suggests that 'person' is an institutional notion. And we find in Stoic ideas that the notion of a person takes on deeper metaphysical meaning as it deepens in social significance. The Stoic idea of all men as citizens of a single City of God combines the ideas of the supreme metaphysical value of the person with the social idea of the person as the bearer of rights and duties.

Hence, in view of this history, it might seem natural to regard 'person' as itself a role-concept.

But to say all this is not to say that 'person' simply names yet another role. If 'person' is a role-concept it is not in the same category as other roles; it cannot be, since it cannot be *chosen*. Thus, it is not that Mr X is a committee member, a teacher, a husband, and a person. The connection between personality and roles is different. To bring this out consider the Greek idea of an *ergon*. The Greeks saw the significance of a craftsman as lying in his function and his virtue in being a good craftsman. For each craft or art there was an end and the craft was designed to further the end. This idea was extended in Aristotle to apply to man as such. He was thought to have an *ergon* or function and a particular virtue. This line of thinking suggests that there is a role or function of man or persons as such. But there may be a category mistake involved here. It is harmless enough to speak of the *ergon* or function or role of a person if by that is meant such things as that persons develop in characteristic ways, carry out some activities better than others, and so on. In short, it is harmless to speak of the role of a person as such if by that is meant only that 'person' is *evaluative* and a different concept from that of 'human being'. But if it means that a given individual human being is an X, Y, Z, *and a person* (where 'person' is put in the same list as the other roles) then the concept of person is distorted, and the concept of role is trivialized. The point of introducing the concept of social role is to stress the often neglected social or impersonal side to morality, to provide a means of conceptualizing the 'what-you-have-got-to-do-as-a-such-and-such'. But if the concept of person is itself analysed in this way there is nothing left to contrast with the impersonal side to morality. It is therefore important in our view to keep a concept of personality irreducible to that of a social role. This point has been much emphasized in Existentialist thinking.

The third objection concedes that there is indeed an irreducible personal aspect to action, and that cognizance must be taken of it if we are to understand action. The objection insists, however, that the personal side to action can still be understood in terms of one or more social sciences. In other words, the third objection allows that we cannot fully understand Miss X's actions as a nurse by spelling out what it is to have the *role* of nurse; we must also know what it is for *Miss X* to be a nurse, and if anything can tell us this the social sciences can, or at least psychology can.

In support of the objection we could refer to the concept of *verstehen*, deployed in the social sciences by many writers. It is not entirely clear what is meant by the term, but it has become the received expression for the kind of understanding of action we aim at when we try to put ourselves on the inside of actions and capture their meaning. Social work theory sometimes uses the (equally unclear) expression *empathy* in attempting to describe the process of understanding an action from the inside.

The difficulty with this, however, is not that these processes of *verstehen* or empathy do not take place, but that it is doubtful whether the sort of understanding coming out of them is properly to be called *scientific*. Scientific understanding, as we have described it, is a matter of fitting events into a pattern, of tracing systematic connections. Moreover, scientific understanding is concerned with things in their generality, with the common or universal properties of things or events. And the same is true of the understanding which the social sciences give of action. They are concerned with what a soldier, an entrepreneur, a dentist, might do, or they are concerned with 'people in stress situations', or the 'one-parent family'. Understanding of this kind, however important, is not the same as the sort involved when we suddenly see, or slowly come to realize, what it is for a specific, named individual, now standing in front of us, to be a soldier, or to be in a specific situation of stress. Understanding of the latter sort is concerned with actions in their *particularity*, with the uniqueness of situations. We might put the point differently by saying that whereas science, including social science, gives us *horizontal* understanding we must in concrete situations supplement this by what we could call *vertical* understanding, the sort of understanding which comes from insight into a personal history.

It does not follow from our claim that this sort of 'vertical' understanding is non-scientific either that it cannot be based on any evidence or that there is no way of testing it. The evidence will be a person's own accounts of how he sees his situation or his problems, and testing one's understanding of his situation is a matter of, for example, gauging his reactions to further questions. A knowledge of social science might be a help here, but it is just as likely to be an impediment because it will encourage the caring worker to see unique individuals and their problems in terms of general categories and labels.

The scientific and the humane in education

There are implications in this for the training of the social worker and nurse, and to a lesser extent for the doctor. When social work moved from the stage of philanthropy, of voluntary societies, to become a profession, those concerned were anxious that it should have its own expertise matching that of other professions. The first move was to base social work practice on the model of the psychoanalyst/patient relationship, and psychology became the main knowledge base for social work. More recently social work has turned to sociology, and now makes use of the new discipline of social administration. We do not wish to suggest that these disciplines are replaceable, but rather wish to point out that they do not provide any guidance or training in the kind of individual judgment of individual situations which we have been emphasizing. How, if at all, can such training be provided?

If at all, it can be provided by a study of literature. God forbid that literature be studied only because it is useful, but a study of literature is *educative* in that it is able to provide insight into the particularity of situations. Whereas science, including social science, proceeds by induction from specific instances to generalized (often idealized) patterns, literature explores unique situations, including conflicts of value of the kind we discussed in earlier chapters, and thereby enables us to acquire insights into universal human predicaments. Study of this sort is as relevant to the career of a social worker or nurse as is the study of highly abstract systematic sociology.

Medicine is different from social work in that its knowledge base must be broadly that of the relevant natural sciences. Nevertheless, as we have stressed, doctors, nurses and dentists treat *patients*, not just diseases, and therefore there ought to be some room in medical education for the humane elements we have been stressing. Moreover, it is doubtful how far academic psychology or sociology make the appropriate contribution to this side of medical education. *Normal* human beings are too diverse in their attitudes and situations to be categorized helpfully by the stereotypes of the social sciences. It may be that the study and discussion of the contemporary novel would be educationally more beneficial to the medical student than the abstractions of social science.

In support of this we can refer first to the importance of health education. A great deal is said of the progress of medical science in this century; for example, many diseases formerly regarded as mass killers have largely vanished – tuberculosis, for example – and this transformation is readily attributed to improved medical care based on medical science. But the improvements have less to do with developments in medical care than with developments in the environment – food, water, air – and with changes in social and cultural attitudes towards disease and life expectancy. If this is the case, and there is a formidable body of literature to support it, then a vital part of the task of doctor, nurse or dentist is that of contributing to the education of patients, and more generally to that of the community and its leaders. Education of this sort requires insights and imagination of the kind best developed *via* a study of the humanities. There is no profit in simply *telling* someone to stop smoking or to lose weight; something much more imaginative is required and the flexibility and insight produced by a study of the humanities are more likely to produce this than a study of social science.

There is a second reason for including elements of a broader humane sort in medical or social work education. The worlds of medicine and social work are highly professionalized, with professional values, professional expertise, and a concern for professional status. It is easy for people working in such worlds to become out of touch with ordinary people, to cease to listen to them, to fail to see themselves as their patients or clients might see them. The cure for this is a deepening self-consciousness, and an enriching of the perception of ordinary human relationships, and these are not to be had from gaining more expertise, but, if they can be had at all, from the wisdom distilled in literature.

5 The meaning of life

Two questions of meaning

Most people occasionally ask themselves questions such as the following: Is there any purpose in life? Is there anything really worthwhile? Is there any real justice in life? Ordinary people ask themselves questions of this sort either in moods of despair – after a bereavement, the failure of long-term plans, a betrayal, the suffering of injustice or indifference, and so on – or in occasional moods of reflection on their own lives or on the world about them. Doctors and social workers have more reason to ask such questions than many of us because they more frequently come up against situations which create despair. Doctors frequently encounter death, and not simply the death of the old but of those who still had much to give when they were struck down; and they can see the misery which death brings to relatives and friends. Social workers encounter the wretchedness of those who are lonely, whose lives are being wasted because of some disadvantage of birth, physical, mental or social; and of those who through drink or other wasting habits have brought misery on themselves. Constant exposure to such situations inevitably generates in the reflective person questions about the ultimate nature of things, about the meaning of life.

Questions of this sort are to be distinguished from those of a different, although clearly overlapping sort. A person might ask himself: What does *my* life add up to? Is there any meaning in my life? Or he might say of himself that when his wife died his life lost all meaning. Now the caring professions, in so far as they deal with the tide of human misery, will encounter people who ask themselves such questions, or of whom such questions can be asked, and it is important for them to have some sort of answer to give. Indeed, doctors, nurses or social workers may well ask such questions about their own lives. It is true that the caring professions are often given as examples of the truly meaningful life, but it is also true that doctors and social workers are brought up against certain limits which encourage the asking of questions of an ultimate kind. For example, there are limits to human skill; some operations are not possible, some savage breasts cannot be soothed. Again, limits are imposed by the intransigence of nature; some diseases are not eradicable because of the changing population of bacteria. For the social worker problems of employment do not seem to be soluble, and conflicts between generations seem to be part of the human situation. Such limits can produce a sense of futility. Despite a lifetime of dedication the problems remain much the same and as a result doubts may be raised in the thoughtful. They may ask themselves what their life adds up to or whether they have been wasting their time. Once again we have the problem of meaningfulness.

In dealing with the problem of meaningfulness it is important to keep apart the two questions mentioned earlier: what is the meaning of life? and, does a given person's life have meaning? There are indeed logical connections between the two questions, but the questions are nevertheless distinct, in that it would be possible to say of someone that his life was meaningless or not worthwhile, while at the same time maintaining that life as a whole was meaningful or worthwhile. Indeed, it would be tempting to hold that affirmative answers to the first set of questions, about life as a whole, are presupposed by the judgments that a given person's life lacks meaning; for what could it mean to say that a given person's life had or lacked meaning unless we had the assurance that life as a whole has meaning? There is some truth in this point but its interpretation requires care. It would be fallacious to argue that because a given person's life was meaningful life as a whole must be, or that because in

one sense life as a whole lacks purpose a given person's life must
lack purpose. There is therefore justification for treating the
questions separately, although we shall expect to find that at a
later stage they must be dealt with together. Let us begin with the
question which, in certain moments of soul-searching, a person
might ask himself: is my life meaningful?

The meaningful life

It is important to notice the complexity of the question of what
constitutes a meaningful life. It is partly a *conceptual* question; a
life will not *count* as meaningful unless certain conditions are
fulfilled. For example, it seems to be part of the very idea of a
meaningful life that what is done in it or with it is for the most
part freely chosen. It is also partly an *empirical* question, for the
entertainment of certain purposes *causes* people to feel that their
lives are meaningful. Indeed, there are specialists experienced in
creating or re-creating a sense of purpose in those who lack one:
for example, medical and social work experts who are familiar
with the stages of bereavement and can help the sufferer to regain
his sense of purpose destroyed by the bereavement. Again, there
is a different sort of social work skill which can help a young
person drifting aimlessly from one sort of petty crime to another.
But not every purpose or aim will serve for the meaningful life,
for we *morally* approve of the meaningful life and therefore withhold the term 'meaningful' from lives which lack purposes of a
certain sort. The purposes which the meaningful life must have
are connected with our moral judgments about the nature of the
self and the activities which express that nature. The three
aspects of the question of the meaningful life are inextricably
connected, in that it is because a person has a moral nature that
the entertainment of certain purposes and not others makes his
life to him seem meaningful, and it is because we recognize this
moral ideal in ourselves that we as language-users restrict the
epithet 'meaningful' to lives which exhibit these moral purposes.
Although we shall not discuss the three aspects of the question
separately the form of our discussion will reflect their influence.

The first condition for the meaningful life is freedom or self-
determination – unless a person feels *he* is in control of what he
does, the direction his life takes, he will not think of his life as

meaningful. This first condition follows from our analysis of the 'distinctive endowment' of a human being as consisting in, among other abilities, the ability to be self-determining (see p.38 ff.); for there must be a conceptual connection between the ideas of the distinctive endowment of a person and the meaningful life. We can begin the discussion of this with the case of the person who is sold into slavery. He desperately wants to follow the life he has been taken from but is compelled to do what the tyrant wants him to do. For such a person life has meaning only in that he might *hope* some day to return, and to the extent that he might preserve some inner integrity of thought although his actions are entirely in the control of the tyrant. This is at least one sort of pitiable situation which medical and social workers are not called on to deal with!

But there are other forms of tyranny with which social workers may be familiar. For example, there are social and economic pressures which for some people are impediments to the meaningful life. In so far as people feel themselves the slaves or victims of some economic structure with which they cannot identify they will feel that their actions are not their own and therefore that their lives lack meaning. The cure for this will be seen by different people in different ways: to the revolutionary the problem calls for the overthrow of the economic system, but to the more cautious or the more pessimistic about utopian ideals (and in this group will be included many medical and social workers), the problem calls for piecemeal reforms, such as the removal of this or that administrative or economic anomaly or injustice, and in the meantime support for those who need it in coming to terms with facts about the society they live in.

So far we have been discussing some of the ways in which constraints of various kinds can be a threat to the meaningful life in that they compel a person to do what he does not want to do, and thus interfere with the exercise of self-determination which we have identified as an essential aspect of our 'distinctive endowment'. But in these cases the person still wants to do what circumstances prevent him from doing, and he can still envisage the possibility of a worthwhile life. There is a much more insidious threat to the meaningful life in the case of the person who comes to *desire* to do what his circumstances constrain him to do, and who can envisage no other form of life. Such a person is compelled by 'mind-forg'd manacles',[1] and he needs help and advice if he is to be freed from them; indeed he needs help if he is to be *made aware* of his imprisonment. There can be various forms of this, and various schools of philosophers have discussed the phenomenon using terminology of different sorts. For example, Marxists see the distinctive feature of human nature as 'consciousness', which for them is construed as a product of history; historical knowledge is self-knowledge. But, for them, when man defines himself in terms of his artefacts – whether they be material products or abstract ideas – he becomes alienated from himself. These reified abstractions, such as religion, the State, capital, deprive men of the possibility of seeing their true predicament and they become trapped in 'false consciousness'. In other words, society is seen as structured by these abstractions, and it follows that no amount of individual effort, or even state intervention, would be adequate to correct this false consciousness. For the Marxist, the only hope for man lies in revolution in which the dominant classes would be overthrown, and with them – and this is the important point for our argument – the economic structure which prevents man from reaching a true understanding of himself and his true wants. When this revolution ushers in the classless society then man will be truly free and his creative energies will be released in worthwhile activities.

It is interesting to note that for the Christian, as for the Marxist, the expression of actual wants in self-determined action is not a sufficient condition of the meaningful life, since for both Christian and Marxist man is blinded by his condition from a perception of his *true* wants. For the Christian, the condition which blinds man to his predicament is his ineradicable tendency to choose his own ends rather than discover God's purpose. This is the condition of sinfulness, and from this condition man cannot escape by his own efforts. Only by the intervention of God in history does man have hope and is he enabled to perceive the pattern which constitutes the meaningful life.

It is possible, however, to accept the distinction between what people in fact may want and what is truly worthwhile or meaningful without being committed to the metaphysical position of either the Marxist or the Christian. For the liberal the distinction could be put in terms of two senses of 'happiness', or 'pleasure', in the language of the nineteenth-century utilitarian thinkers such as J.S. Mill. The orthodox utilitarians had argued that one pleasure could be better than another only if it were quantitatively greater, but Mill argues that, quite apart from questions of quantity, one pleasure can be qualitatively better than another, the criterion being the preference of those who have experienced both the pleasures in question. We are told that a being with higher faculties requires more to make him happy, but that he would not on that account change his place with the fool even for the fool's satisfaction. 'It is better to be a human being dissatisfied than a pig satisfied; better to be Socrates dissatisfied than a fool satisfied. And if the fool, or the pig, are of a different opinion, it is because they only know their own side of the question.'[2] The qualitative criterion, then, is the preference of experienced judgment.

Now if Mill's distinction is taken at its face value, and interpreted in the customary hedonistic context, it is not defensible. It is true that if we want to know which of two items is the better for a certain purpose, or if we want to know whether a smallpox vaccination is more or less painful than a penicillin injection, we may ask the person who has experience of both. But this method does not work for a qualitative distinction between pleasures, since we all find pleasure in doing whatever we can do well. Socrates may say that arguing produces a pleasure qualitatively superior to that of wallowing in the mud, but the pig may reply that Socrates has not really given wallowing a chance, has not appreciated its finer points. Hence, assuming a hedonistic conception of the ultimate end, we cannot draw the qualitative distinction in a defensible manner.

But consider Mill's views of the ultimate end as they are expressed in *On Liberty*.[3] In the third chapter Mill criticizes the common modes of thinking on the grounds that 'individual spontaneity is hardly recognized as having any intrinsic worth, or deserving any regard on its own account.' In this passage Mill is explicitly admitting that something other than happiness is intrinsically desirable – individuality. He then goes on to praise a doctrine of self-development or self-realization, expressed in the words of the German philosopher Wilhelm von Humboldt, namely that the ultimate end for man is 'the highest and most harmonious development of his powers to a complete and consistent whole'. The connection between 'individuality' (or 'originality', as Mill also calls it) and the self-development doctrine lies in Mill's belief that to be original in living, to be an individual, is to develop oneself by using 'the qualities which are the distinctive endowment of a human being' in the choice of one's own plan of life. The *On Liberty* conception of the end, then, is self-development through the development of individuality.

There are even faint hints of this view in *Utilitarianism*. Mill gives the orthodox utilitarian account of the ultimate end in ch. 2, but when he answers the objections that happiness is unattainable, he seems to be suggesting, although he is not explicit about it, that the ultimate end is the full development of human potentialities. Thus, he writes that a 'cultivated mind ... finds sources of inexhaustible interest in all that surrounds it; in the objects of nature, the achievements of art, the imaginations of poetry ...'. Again, when he is discussing 'the possibility of giving to the service of humanity ... both the psychological power and the social efficacy of a religion' his fear is that such a procedure might be so effective as to 'interfere unduly with human freedom and individuality'.[4] These passages suggest that ripples of the *On Liberty* doctrines remained to disturb the hedonistic surface of *Utilitarianism*. And certainly in terms of the *On Liberty* conception of the end the qualitative distinction can be re-stated in a way which makes better sense.

In terms of the *On Liberty* doctrine, Mill's qualitative distinction can be put as a distinction not between pleasures but between activities. The point of the distinction is now that some activities are preferable to others. But why should we prefer some activities to others? Why should we prefer poetry to pushpin? The answer is that poetry, being richer and more complex and therefore impinging on a greater area of human experience, is more likely to lead to self-development. There are, of course, people who prefer pushpin to poetry, but Mill would say that they are liable to be 'unoriginal' people whose individuality has never been developed. If we re-interpret the qualitative distinction in this way, its criterion emerges as the advice of those who, like Socrates, are highly developed individuals. Thus Mill writes, 'It really is of importance, not only what men do, but also what manner of men they are that do it.'[5] On this interpretation Mill's distinction seems to be a viable one: a higher value can be set on some activities than on others, not for the amount of pleasure they produce but for their ability to deepen a person's individuality and so to help him to develop himself.

It may be argued, however, that Mill's two conceptions of the end really come to the same thing, for the justification for commending self-development is simply that it will produce more pleasure for the 'self' concerned. To commend an activity because it is rich and complex and therefore likely to conduce more to self-development is merely a roundabout way of saying that it will produce a greater quantity of pleasure for certain people over a long period. Now Mill would not want to deny that a person in the process of developing his potentialities is also likely to experience on the whole a greater quantity of pleasure than one who simply abides by convention. But the justification for making self-development the end does not lie in the pleasure which may accompany its attainment. Nor does Mill think that it does, for he puts forward justification of another sort. He writes that human nature 'is not a machine to be built after a model ... but a tree, which requires to grow and develop itself on all sides, according to the tendency of the inward forces which make it a living thing.'[6] Again, he praises the 'Greek ideal of self-development', and suggests that if human beings develop what is individual in themselves they will become 'a noble and beautiful object of contemplation'. In these and other passages Mill seems to be operating with a conception – partly moral and partly aesthetic – of human nature as something which may, more or less, 'flourish'. The argument, which is at least as old as Socrates, is that it is somehow incumbent on us as human beings to act in ways which will make our natures 'flourish'. This is what Mill seems to have in mind when he regards the moral end as self-development, and although it is not clearly worked out in his thought, the conception does not appear to be a hedonistic one.

The point in all this, as it affects our concerns, is that in most traditions of thought there is a distinction between what a person *happens* to want at a given historical moment, and what he *truly wants*, what constitutes his true happiness or interests and is therefore worthwhile. While moral and political traditions vary in the importance they attach to being able to do what one in fact wants – being able to exercise self-determination – most traditions of thought see the *meaningful* life as being necessarily connected with the pursuit of true happiness or the worthwhile, differing only in their conceptions of the worthwhile life, or in their conceptions of the nature of the self. For the liberal-democratic tradition, typified by J.S. Mill, the meaningful life is that in which the exercise of purposiveness or self-determination is directed towards those rich and complex ends which are worthwhile in that they realize the potentialities, the capacities and inclinations, integral to developing and extending the self. For the individual the ideal is here the rich and complex self, originality in living, and for society it is a variety in which the differences between people are given scope and encouragement.

It might be objected that self-realization so conceived might conflict with the pursuit of the good of others. But this is not the case. It will be remembered that the characteristic human endowment – the raw material for self-realization – contains not only the ability to be self-determining or purposive but also the ability to stand back from one's own concerns and regulate one's conduct in terms of ideals seen as valid for all men. To restrain one's self in the interests of other selves is therefore at the same time to be developing one's self. The self is a moral self.

A question might be raised as to how far the process of self-realization must be self-conscious. Could a person develop his abilities without being aware that this was what he was doing? Can self-development be unreflective? Socrates said that the unreflective life was not worth living. Was he right in this? Here we may helpfully consider the analogous question of whether the person who feels no fear and does not reflect on what he is doing is truly courageous. The answer to this question is partly a matter of decision as to how to use the word 'courage', but we can say that the person who experiences fear but still chooses to act as reason and duty dictate is exhibiting courage in a more truly human mode than that exhibited by the unreflective person. Likewise the person who consciously chooses to follow a certain pattern in his actions is exhibiting a more truly meaningful life than the person who unreflectively follows the same pattern. This is more clearly true of meaningful behaviour than courageous behaviour, because the meaningful is necessarily connected with choice in the way in which the courageous is not. It is therefore a conceptual truth that the meaningful life is the reflective life; it is the reflective pursuit of self-development and the good of others.

It should be noted at this point that the analysis of the meaningful life we are suggesting would be rejected by two schools of philosophers, both of which have been influential in shaping the ideas of scientists and social scientists. The first of these is the materialistic-mechanistic school, of which the modern source is Hobbes in the seventeenth century.[7] According to this view, human nature is simply matter in motion, and human thought and action can all ultimately be explained in terms of the laws of physics and chemistry. A powerful twentieth-century form of this view is to be found in behavioural psychology. Influenced originally by the work of Pavlov on conditioned responses, behavioural psychologists have developed complicated theories based on concepts such as 'drive' which can be seen as in some way bridging the gap between purposive models of human behaviour and purely physiological models. We do not propose to take the discussion of the many complexities of the sophisticated modern versions of this theory further than we took them in our previous chapter, but it is clear that the theory is not compatible with the conception of the meaningful life we have suggested.[8] If human beings are in the end complex conditioned-response mechanisms then the appropriate way to treat them is by means of rewards, punishments and tranquillizers, and effort spent on trying to get them to understand their situation, to reflect on it and to *choose* their activities in the light of their reflection, is wasted; it is irrelevant to the model of man being used.

There is no doubt that a great deal of modern medical and social work practice is based on this philosophical model of man. It is indeed obviously possible to keep large numbers of people happy, in the sense of subjectively contented, by the continual administration of some tranquillizing drug, and perhaps that is all that can be done with some mental or social disorders. But a life of this quality could not be considered *meaningful*, for the reasons that its actions and attitudes are not really the person's own, but are causally induced by the drugs. Again, a person could live a perfectly contented life of conformity to social pressures, of doing what others expect, of doing the done thing. Such a life need not be the worst possible (although, as we shall see, Sartre and other Existentialists would say that it was) but it would not be a meaningful life. It often takes a personal shock to force a person to review his life, to see it in a wider context, and when this process begins then the question of meaningfulness becomes relevant. The happy life, in the sense of the subjectively contented life, is therefore distinct from the meaningful life, in that the former need not be, whereas the latter must be, *chosen* (not induced) and self-conscious. The happy life in this sense is the nearest analogue to meaningfulness in the mechanistic view of human nature.

At the opposite extreme to the views of mechanism are those of a school of philosophers who were influential in the period 1940-60; and while the movement is no longer so active among professional philosophers it is still influential in schools of social work and psychiatry. We refer to Existentialism.[9] According to Existentialists there cannot be such a process as 'self-realization' or 'self-development', because there is no 'essential self' to be realized. Human beings are like hollow tubes and have no goals which they ought to aim at in their lives. The only characteristic which defines a person is his absolute freedom, and the nearest analogue to moral wrong-doing is his refusal to exercise this freedom in authentic choice, conforming instead to the expectations which others have of him. Someone who denies his freedom in this way has become like a *thing*, following causal patterns, and not like a person who can act in the mode of free choice.

Now we do not propose here to argue against Existentialism, or to develop further its interesting ideas. For someone who adopted such a standpoint the meaningful life would be the life in which free choice was exercised regardless of what was chosen. From our standpoint, however, whereas the free choice of a life-style, or at least the conscious acceptance of one, is a *necessary* condition of the meaningful life, we reject the view that it is *sufficient*. It seems to us to matter *what* is chosen, and we are asserting that for meaningfulness what must be chosen are the activities which realize the self. As we have seen, the concepts of health and welfare are concerned in different ways with the 'wholeness' of a person. But 'wholeness' is a dynamic idea, a matter of *becoming* rather than just *being*, and the terms of 'self-realization' or 'self-development' express the idea of the 'becoming' of human personality.

The importance of the concept of 'self-realization' is recognized by social workers to the extent that the first principle of the profession of social work is stated as follows:

Basic to the profession of social work is the recognition of the value and dignity of every individual human being, irrespective of origin, status, sex, age, belief or contribution to society. The profession accepts a responsibility to encourage and facilitate the self-realization of the individual person with due regard for the interests of others.[10]

In discussing 'self-realization' we have therefore been concerned with a central concept of the caring professions, and this is to be expected if self-realization is indeed the key to the meaningful life.

The meaning of life

The *meaningful life* (we claim) is the self-realized life. Turning now to the idea of the *meaning of life* we can note an important initial difference between the two ideas. It is that one can speak of a 'meaningful life' without implying that there is something that the meaningful life means, or that anything is meant by a life that is meaningful. The meaningful life is simply the life with significance, the life worth leading. On the other hand, to speak of 'the meaning of life' is to imply that there is something that life means, or that someone means something by life, just as to speak of the meaning of a hand signal is to imply that there is something that the hand signal means or that someone means something by the hand signal. But what sense can be attached to the ideas that life means something, or that someone means something by life? Sense can be attached to the idea if it is placed in a religious context. Thus God can be said to have meant something by life and what He meant, His purpose, is what life means.

We can connect the meaning of life on this interpretation with our earlier analysis of the meaningful life by saying that the meaningful life will be that which embodies or reflects God's purpose. It will be meaningful in that, since God created our nature with a purpose in His mind, the life which fulfils His purpose will be the self-realized life, and therefore the life experienced as meaningful. This account has an ancient religious tradition behind it, and it appeals as practical belief. We might say that in terms of this view the 'meaningful life' becomes assimilated to the 'meaning of life' in the sense that the latter

concept must be used to explain or give significance to the
former. But although the meaning of life is here thought to lie
beyond life as lived, someone holding philosophical beliefs of this
sort is not obliged by them to turn away from the everyday world
and its concerns. Rather he will see in the carrying out of
everyday duties a significance which attaches a profound
meaning to them. This point of view is beautifully expressed in a
poem by the seventeenth-century poet George Herbert:[11]

THE ELIXIR

Teach me, my God and King,
In all things Thee to see,
And what I do in any thing
To do it as for Thee.

Not rudely, as a beast,
To runne into an action;
But still to make Thee prepossest,
And give it his perfection.

A man that looks on glasse,
On it may stay his eye;
Or if he pleaseth, through it passe,
and then the heav'n espie.

All may of Thee partake:
Nothing can be so mean
Which with his tincture, 'for Thy sake,'
Will not grow bright and clean.

A servant with this clause
Makes drudgery divine;
Who sweeps a room as for Thy laws
Makes that and th' action fine.

This is the famous stone
That turneth all to gold;
For that which God doth touch and own
Cannot for lesse be told.

According to this view, then, life as a whole has a meaning, but
the meaning of life lies beyond life; it is something towards which
life points but which transcends life.

Characteristically this is a religious philosophy of the world, but secular versions are possible. In secular versions the 'Kingdom of Heaven' is some future state of society, hope of which gives meaning to otherwise empty human activities. This future state could be a classless society from which economic competition has disappeared, or a pure Nordic civilization. The ideal, whatever it is, nevertheless has the same features as the religious version; the 'meaning of life' is perceived in the arrival of some far-off event towards which everything is directed and hope of which gives meaning to an otherwise futile life.

Philosophies of this sort, religious or secular, have a number of disadvantages. They depend on many premises all of which can be disputed and for which there is no conclusive argument. Thus, to take the religious version, it requires acceptance of the following premises: that there exists a Creator; that He has purposes for human beings; and that human beings will have meaningful lives by fulfilling these purposes. We shall not enter into discussion of these premises since argument about them constitutes a branch of philosophy in itself. It should be noted, however, that such transcendent views of the meaning of life have a disadvantage which might make them unacceptable even to some religious believers. It is that according to them the meaning of life lies beyond life itself. In other words, human life with all its apparent richness has no significance *in itself*; it has meaning only in so far as it points *beyond itself*. Indeed, extreme forms of the transcendent view turn into world-rejecting asceticism. But not all those who have religious beliefs would want to reject human life quite so firmly.

As an alternative to such views there has therefore grown up since the seventeenth century a religious philosophy which portrays the meaning of life as lying in life itself. This approach has its origins in Renaissance humanism and its tradition can be traced through Kant to some modern theologians such as Paul Tillich. According to this philosophy the meaning of life, its significance, lies in the manner in which life is lived. The meaning of life is something experienced in whole-hearted *commitment* to the claims of life. In the sphere of morality, for instance, those people know the meaning of life who commit themselves unsparingly to the service of others. Again, the meaning of life can be experienced in a commitment to art; in being profoundly moved by great music one experiences the meaning of life. The 'meaning of life', then, is construed as a quality of intensity in the living of it. To put it grammatically, the 'meaning' of life on the first interpretation was a substantive prepositionally connected with 'life', but on this interpretation it is an adverb, a manner of living.

An important question which requires to be considered in the development of this view concerns the particular sense of 'know' involved when it is said that in certain sorts of commitment one 'knows' the meaning of life. To put the question in another way, if we turn to some wise person for advice, because he knows 'what it's all about', or what the meaning of life is, what does he know, and in what sense of 'know'? He might be said to *know that* certain things are the case. In other words, he might be said to possess a certain number of true facts about the world and human behaviour. But while he will need to have some of this sort of knowledge to know the meaning of life, the extent to which it is necessary can be exaggerated; Tolstoy's peasants are depicted as simple men who, although ignorant, know the meaning of life. No doubt Tolstoy sentimentalizes his peasants, but they remain convincing for all that. Does the wise man *know how* to live? Does he possess certain skills? No doubt he does, but it is not in respect of any expertise that a person might be said to know the meaning of life.

More relevant to this question is a third kind of knowledge – *knowledge by acquaintance* – as when one knows a person. Sometimes knowing a person can be a superficial matter, but where deep friendship or love are concerned there is a new dimension in the relationship and therefore in the knowledge involved. It is knowledge analogous to this, a knowledge which involves commitment, which is claimed when someone 'knows the meaning of life'. Consider another analogy. Suppose a gifted child plays a profound piece of music. The performance need not be unmusical – the child may well observe the dynamics of the music in a sensitive way – but we might nevertheless feel dissatisfied with it. The child, we might say, does not understand what the music is 'all about'. A mature performer by contrast has the kind of *commitment* to the music which comes from richer human experience, and in the sense in which he knows what the music is about we have an analogy with 'knowing' the meaning of life.

Plato in the *Republic* provides an illuminating discussion of this sort of knowledge when he examines 'knowledge of the Good'.[12] He compares the Good to the sun which sheds light on all things and both attracts and dazzles human beings. Although there are many degrees of knowledge in Plato's scheme he believes that the highest form is a kind of direct acquaintance which carries a commitment with it. By looking at the sun one is enabled to see all things, which previously were seen dimly and in distorted forms. Moreover, knowledge of this sort is inexhaustible and relevant to all situations. Returning to the analogy of friendship we might say that just as knowledge of a close friend is not exhausted by any list of statements about the friend, so knowledge of the meaning of life is not exhausted by any set of statements about life.

How then are we to characterize knowledge of the meaning of life? Pulling together the strands of the discussion we can say that it seems possible to be led to know (in the sense of 'be acquainted with') the meaning of life by a certain manner of living it. It is less necessary to have rich and varied experience for this knowledge than it is to be able to see life as a whole; to be detached from life while at the same time being committed wholeheartedly to the living of it. Moreover, if knowing the meaning of life on this approach is living in a certain way we can say further that the 'certain way' is the way of the meaningful or the self-realized life. In other words, knowing the meaning of life on this interpretation is the very same as leading a meaningful life. Just as on the transcendent interpretation of the 'meaning of life' the concept of the 'meaningful life' was assimilated to that of the 'meaning of life', so on this 'immanent' interpretation the 'meaning of life' is assimilated to the 'meaningful life'.

We have discussed the 'immanent' interpretation of the 'meaning of life' in secular terms, but it can also be regarded as implied by the Christian message. For example, in the parable of the sheep and the goats God is described as a king passing judgment. He says to the righteous, 'I was an-hungered and ye gave me meat; I was thirsty, and ye gave me drink; I was a stranger, and ye took me in . . . .' The righteous are puzzled by this and ask when they did these things. God replies, 'Inasmuch as ye have done it unto one of the least of these my brethren, ye have done it unto me.'[13] The point here is not that the hungry were fed *for the sake of* some other or future religious value; they were fed for the sufficient reason that they were people who needed feeding. The point of the parable is to assert that this total commitment to the needs of other people is also, in virtue of that very fact, a religious commitment. This parable is, of course, concerned with morality, but we can find warrant in the Gospels for generalizing the idea. Thus, Jesus says, 'I am come that they might have life and have it more abundantly.'[14] The point here may be to direct us to the meaning of life via the meaningful life seen as intensity in living. Our concern in these brief remarks, however, is not to advocate a religious view of life, or one interpretation of the Christian Gospels rather than another, but simply to suggest tentatively that those who hold a Christian viewpoint still have some scriptural warrant for seeing the meaning of life as lying in a quality of living life, or in the meaningful life.

Conclusion

Our analysis of the concepts of the meaningful life and the meaning of life, and of the connection between them, sums up our philosophy of the caring professions. One of our themes has been that in different ways the concepts of health and welfare are connected, both being aspects of a single value judgment about the nature of a person, or about 'wholeness', and about the physical, mental, social, economic and environmental conditions necessary to foster the growth of personality. We have developed these ideas in various ways, and have tried to show how they lead to the conclusion that the self-realized life is the meaningful life. Although the idea of the meaning of life can be understood in various rational and appealing ways as lying in some world-transcending state of affairs we have preferred to understand it as a manner of living life; those people know the meaning of life who commit themselves to it with intensity. In other words, those know the meaning of life who lead meaningful or self-realizing lives.

Now if 'knowing the meaning of life' is not any kind of propositional knowledge or any kind of skill, then it cannot require any kind of expertise and it is therefore not anything which can be taught to students or administered to patients and clients. But if the caring professions are aiming at 'wholeness' in their dealings

with patients and clients then they must somehow both themselves have and be able to impart this sense. How can this be
done? It cannot be taught, but it can be 'caught'. In other words a
sense of what life is about, of what makes it worth living, can be
communicated via an inspiring teacher, a dedicated GP, an act of
friendship, a sympathetic and attentive social worker. The com-
munication of this can sometimes succeed in doing for someone
what expertise has failed to do. For example, social workers are
anxious, and rightly so, to develop a professional expertise and
are sometimes scornful of the efforts of those who lack their training. Yet it is a fact that the Salvation Army can sometimes
succeed with an alcoholic or recidivist when expertise has failed.
The secret of the success is presumably the selfless devotion and
love, or the personal qualities and commitment, of the Salvation-
ist which have 'got through' where expertise has failed.

Medicine even more than social work has become a matter of
technical expertise, the benefits of which are manifest and much
celebrated. But the temptation is to shelter behind expertise,
because it is easier to be a technical expert to a patient, adopting
the appropriate objective attitude of the technician, than to
confront him in a personal relationship of equality with the
strains which that may involve. It might be objected that the
average doctor does not require the qualities of personality we
have been discussing, for his problems are almost entirely those
calling for expertise. How can qualities of personality, a sense of
the wider perspectives, the meaning of life, be of assistance to the
overworked doctor confronted with aches and pains, depression,
skin disorders and so on? The answer is that many of these
disorders are now thought to be caused by anxieties, inadequacies
and general problems of life which the patient desperately wants
to talk about. Or he makes his aches and pains the *occasion* of a
visit to a doctor when it is really a bereavement or other 'arrest of
life' which he would like to be made to discuss. For the doctor to
hide behind a white coat and box of pills is for him to take the
easy way out from a more human confrontation (although no
doubt busy doctors could be forgiven for taking the easy way out).

At this point it might be objected by either medical or social
workers that whereas it is indeed an evasion to reach for a box of
pills when it is a discussion of a bereavement that is more appropriate, there is another sort of expertise appropriate for such

situations. For instance, if our example is of bereavement, then a doctor or social worker familiar with the systematic studies of grief and bereavement conducted by, say, Dr Colin Murray Parkes[15] would be better able to cope than someone lacking such knowledge. Now this is likely to be true and we must not be thought to be denying or underestimating the importance of the social sciences for our understanding of human behaviour. We said as much in chapter 4. But we also stressed that knowledge of behaviour patterns in general terms is not sufficient for understanding the unique case in front of us. Indeed, it is the wrong *sort* of understanding (see pp.139-40). Moreover, and this is here the crucial point, what is required from the doctor or social worker is not only intellectual or scientific understanding, but the sort of compassionate help and advice which one human being experienced in life's miseries can give another. This does not come from *having knowledge* (however desirable that may be) but from *being a certain kind of person*.

Moreover, 'to be a certain kind of person' does not mean here to see oneself as different from, far less superior to, others. On the contrary, it means being able to communicate, verbally and non-verbally, as one human being to another. To return to the example of the Salvation Army, it is plausible to say that one reason for their success is that they do not see their alcoholics as people different from themselves with problems – 'Tell me about your problems!' – but rather see themselves and their alcoholics as equally sinners. The danger of professionalism or expertise in the caring professions is that it prevents the recognition of what is valid in the Salvation Army approach – that there are truths which can be communicated in the quality of living life but which cannot be stated in propositions.

Now if this is true and important for the caring professions, or at least some aspects of them (for obviously it is not applicable to the neuro-surgeon about to carry out an operation which requires great technical expertise), it has implications for the education of the caring professions. To be able to adopt a broader, humane attitude to the problems of the caring professions requires exposure to some non-technical disciplines and some familiarity with the value-bases of health and welfare. The point of this is not to weigh down the already over-burdened student with yet another body of knowledge with its attendant examinations, but to give him the opportunity to cultivate what is his as an ordinary agent: the ability to make informed non-technical judgments about the problems of life and to communicate a sense of the meaning of life within a relationship of equality with patients and clients.

Appendix:
Ethics, morals
and moral philosophy

Many scientists and men of action have little sympathy with discussions of words, regarding all such as easy to settle – 'Look it up in the dictionary!' – or as trivial – 'Just word-chopping!'. But disputes about words cannot always be settled so easily, since dictionaries may well just record the ambiguities which have occasioned the disputes; and they are often anything but trivial, since the meanings we attach to words certainly influence, and may even determine, our perceptions of the world or our values. Indeed, in some cases there is no clear distinction between changing one's view of the meanings of words and changing one's view of the facts. These points are illustrated by the confusions surrounding the words 'ethics' and 'morals' as these words are used in medical discussion; the points could also be illustrated by examples from social work discussions.

The first use of 'ethics' we shall note is that in which it is synonymous with 'morals'. In this sense of the term an 'ethical judgment' is the judgment of an ordinary moral agent about moral right and wrong, about what someone morally ought or ought not to do, about whether or not someone behaved fairly, or about whether or not someone is a morally good person. In this sense we might say that a certain question is a matter of ethics rather than of politics.

But although 'ethics' and 'morals' can be co-extensive in their areas of application, there are also, second, uses of 'ethics' and 'morals' in terms of which they refer to roughly distinguishable areas *within* 'ethics' or 'morals' in the first sense. Thus, in popular speech the term 'morals' has become narrowed to matters of sexual behaviour, whereas high-minded people who are aware that there are problems of conduct other than sexual ones have pre-empted the word 'ethics' to refer to them. In terms of this distinction we find that the politician who tells us lies is deemed (if caught at it) 'unethical', whereas his mistress who is caught at it (no need to say what) is deemed to have 'loose morals'. In short, 'ethics' and 'morals' can refer to two different areas of ordinary morality in the first sense.

Different again, and of greatest interest to the medical profession, is the use of 'ethics' in the expression 'professional ethics', of which medical ethics is an important branch. All codes of professional ethics embody three main components: standards of *professional competence*; standards of *professional integrity*; accepted *professional procedures*, or, in a broad sense, 'etiquette'. A professional code of this sort can acquire the force of moral imperatives in our first sense. The moral duties of life which are for most people diffused over many areas and activities have for the dedicated caring worker a sharper focus, and in so far as they are more sharply defined they can have a degree of strength which outweighs all other claims on him. Seen in this way professional ethics are a source of inspiration and a profession becomes a vocation or a calling. Professional ethics can thus be ordinary morality at its finest, and the third sense of 'ethics' becomes a specialized case of the first.

It is possible, however, and perhaps it is not uncommon, for the institutional side of professional ethics to become dominant. When that happens the emphasis is placed on professional procedures, procedures which may of course be justifiable but can seem artificial or just plain comic, as when it is a matter of precedence in the ward round. This gives us a fourth sense of 'ethics', when the term acquires a specific content which refers to codified procedures, but lacks the prescriptive force of morality. An example of 'ethics' used in this descriptive, procedural sense can be found in the reaction of the Ethical Committee of the British Medical Association to the virginity tests alleged to have been carried out on Asian immigrant women at Heathrow Airport. A spokesman for the BMA is reported as having said that while such tests may have been morally wrong there was nothing unethical about them.[1] Presumably the meaning of this is that there was nothing in the codified procedures of the BMA which could be interpreted as ruling out such tests. 'Ethics' in this procedural, quasi-legal sense is distinct from 'morals' or 'morality' in the first sense, as we can see if we consider that it is possible to decide by a majority vote what will or will not count as *ethical* in this sense, whereas an action or a practice cannot be made *morally* right or wrong by a majority decision or piece of legislation. Thus, it is logically possible, and perhaps not uncommon, for someone to dissent on moral grounds from a decree that a given practice is ethically right or wrong in the descriptive sense. For example, it might be decided by the Ethical Committee of the BMA or other such body that providing AID for lesbians is ethically wrong or right, but a doctor or social worker might well dissent from such a decree on moral grounds, just as we might object morally to certain laws although they have been enacted by Parliament. Ethics, in this sense of codified procedures, does not in itself, then, have moral force, although clearly any member of a profession has a moral duty to consider the codified procedures of his profession and to act on them unless he can show good reason why he ought not – just as a citizen has a general moral duty to obey the law of the land and may dissent only if he can show morally good grounds for his dissent.

'Ethics', finally, is often used to refer to that branch of philosophy also called 'moral philosophy'. Thus, philosophers write books with titles such as *The Methods of Ethics* or *Principia Ethica*, and such books are concerned with the philosophical study of the principles governing man's life in society. Ethics in this sense is a theoretical, second-order study of practical, first-order morality or ethics, and its aim is to bring about an intellectual understanding of the nature of moral action and judgment. It does not follow from this that moral philosophy as a theoretical study has no relevance to practical morality. Perhaps an analogy from music may help here. The study of the form and structure of music is a purely theoretical study, but nevertheless a performer will have a better overall grasp of the music he is playing if he has this theoretical knowledge. There are of course musicians with an intuitive insight into the music they are playing, just as there are ordinary moral agents with an intuitive insight into moral situations, but it remains true that most people will have a more informed awareness of morality if they have some theoretical grasp of the principles underlying it.

It will be clear from the foregoing that discussions of at least some words can be both controversial – not to be settled by appeals to dictionaries or stipulations – and important, since confusions over the meaning of 'ethics' (for example) may lead to serious misunderstandings among members of a profession or between a profession and the general public.

References

Chapter 1 The value base of the caring professions

1 Cf. Central Council for Education and Training in Social Work, *Values in Social Work*, CCETSW Paper 13 (London, CCETSW, 1976).

2 We have discussed the concept of an 'aim' (as intrinsic, extrinsic, etc.,) in R.S. Downie, Eileen M. Loudfoot, Elizabeth Telfer, *Education and Personal Relationships* (London, Methuen, 1974), ch.1.

3 See, for example, David Watson, 'Welfare Rights and Human Rights', *Journal of Social Policy*, vol.6, part 1, 1977; Angus McKay, 'Charity and the Welfare State' in Noel Timms and David Watson (eds), *Philosophy in Social Work* (London, Routledge & Kegan Paul, 1978).

4 J.R. Rees, *Mental Health and the Offender* (London, Clarke Hall Fellowship, 1947), p.6.

5 Antony Flew, *Crime or Disease?* (London, Macmillan, 1973).

6 ibid.

7 David Hume, *An Enquiry Concerning the Principles of Morals*, ed. by L.A. Selby-Bigge (Oxford, Clarendon Press, 2nd edn. 1902), Appendix 1.

8 J.S. Mill, *On Liberty*, ed. by Mary Warnock (London, Collins, 1962), ch. 3.

9 Plato, *Republic*, trans. by B. Jowett (London, Sphere Books, 1970), pp.444-5.

Chapter 2   The principles governing the caring professions

1 We have argued for this principle at length in R.S. Downie and Elizabeth Telfer, *Respect for Persons* (London, Allen & Unwin, 1969).
2 For the expression 'distinctive endowment' see J.S. Mill, *On Liberty*, ed. by Mary Warnock (London, Collins, 1962), p.187.
3 For a full discussion of the rights of animals see S.R.L. Clark, *The Moral Status of Animals* (Oxford, Clarendon Press, 1977).
4 Jonathan Glover, *Causing Death and Saving Lives* (Harmondsworth, Penguin Books, 1977), p.82.
5 American Declaration of Independence.
6 Mill, op. cit., p.135.
7 For the distinction between rights of action and rights of recipience see D.D. Raphael, 'Human Rights, Old and New', in D.D. Raphael (ed.), *Political Theory and the Rights of Man* (London, Macmillan, 1967).
8 Mill, op. cit., p.135.
9 See, for example, M.H. Pappworth, *Human Guinea Pigs* (London, Routledge & Kegan Paul, 1967); Rt. Hon. The Lord Platt, 'Human Guinea Pigs', in *Morals and Medicine* (London, BBC, 1970); A.V. Campbell, *Moral Dilemmas in Medicine* (Edinburgh, Churchill Livingstone, 1975), pp.153-61 and references there.

Chapter 3   The politics of the caring professions

1 Adam Smith, *The Wealth of Nations*, ed. by E. Cannan (New York, Random House, 1937), p.437.
2 Plato, *Republic*, trans. by B. Jowett (London, Sphere Books, 1970), Book I.
3 Smith, op. cit., p.735.
4 ibid., p.738.
5 ibid., Book 1, ch.11.
6 P.H. Wicksteed, *The Commonsense of Political Economy*, ed. by L. Robbins (London, George Routledge, 1933), pp.174-80. We are indebted to Professor T. Wilson of Glasgow University for introducing us to the works of Wicksteed.
7 For a discussion of the nature of economic relations see W.D. Lamont, *The Value Judgement* (Edinburgh University Press, 1955).

8 Kant, *Groundwork of the Metaphysic of Morals* (London, Hutchinson, 1948), ch. 2.

9 We have discussed the nature of relationships and attitudes in more detail in R.S. Downie, Eileen M. Loudfoot and Elizabeth Telfer, *Education and Personal Relationships* (London, Methuen, 1974).

10 The terms 'objective' and 'reactive' as applied to attitudes in this sense were introduced by P.F. Strawson in 'Freedom and Resentment', *Proceedings of the British Academy* vol.XLVIII, 1962. We have discussed the terms in Downie, Loudfoot and Telfer, op. cit.

11 Our discussion is based on R.F. Stalley, 'Non-judgemental Attitudes' in Noel Timms and David Watson (eds) *Philosophy in Social Work* (London, Routledge & Kegan Paul, 1978).

12 Our discussion here is based on Elizabeth Telfer, 'Justice, Welfare and Health Care', *Journal of Medical Ethics*, vol.2, no.3, September 1976.

Chapter 4   The knowledge base of the caring professions

1 Cf. Descartes, *Meditations* (London, Dent, Everyman Library, 1st edn 1912), II.

2 For an extended argument for the logical and metaphysical priority of the 'thing', see P.F. Stawson, *Individuals* (London, Methuen, 1959).

3 Our discussion of the nature of scientific laws, experiments, etc., has been much influenced by E. Nagel, *The Structure of Science* (London, Routledge & Kegan Paul, 1961); W. Kneale, *Probability and Induction*, (London, Oxford University Press, 1949); S. Toulmin, *The Philosophy of Science* (London, Hutchinson, 1953).

4 Robert Boyle, *The Sceptical Chymist* (London, Dent), p.559.

5 Galileo, *Dialogues Concerning Two New Sciences*, trans. by H. Crew and A. de Salvio (New York, Dover Publications, 1914), Third Day.

6 We have discussed the concept of a social role more fully in R.S. Downie, Eileen M. Loudfoot and Elizabeth Telfer, *Education and Personal Relationships* (London, Methuen, 1974).

Chapter 5   The meaning of life

1 The expression 'mind-forg'd manacles' comes from William Blake's poem 'London' contained in his *Songs of Innocence and Experience* (London, Oxford University Press, 1927).

2 J.S. Mill, *Utilitarianism*, ed. by Mary Warnock (London, Collins, 1962), ch.2.
3 J.S. Mill, *On Liberty*, ed. by Mary Warnock (London, Collins, 1962), ch.3.
4 Mill, *Utilitarianism*, ch.2.
5 Mill, *On Liberty*, ch.3.
6 ibid.
7 Thomas Hobbes, *Leviathan*, ed. by J.P. Plamenatz (London, Collins, 1962).
8 Cf. M. Shaw and others, 'Ethical Implications of a Behavioural Approach' in D. Jehu (ed.), *Behaviour Modification in Social Work* (London, Wiley Inter-Science, 1972).
9 See J.-P. Sartre, *Being and Nothingness*, trans. by H.E. Barnes (London, Methuen, 1969).
10 British Association of Social Workers, *A Code of Ethics for Social Work*, Discussion Paper no.2 (London, BASW, 1972).
11 George Herbert, 'The Elixir', from *The Temple* (London, Oxford University Press, 1907).
12 Plato, *Republic*, trans. by B. Jowett (London, Sphere Books, 1970), Books VI-VII.
13 St Matthew's Gospel, ch.25, 31-46.
14 St John's Gospel, ch.10, 10.
15 C.M. Parkes, *Bereavement* (Harmondsworth, Penguin Books, 1975).

Appendix

1 *World Medicine* (March 10, 1979), p.99.

Recommended reading

The classical sources of the philosophy we have put forward can be found in the following works, which are published in many editions:

Plato, *Republic*.

Aristotle, *Nicomachean Ethics*.

Kant, *Groundwork of the Metaphysic of Morals*.

J.S. Mill, *Utilitarianism* and *On Liberty*.

The following are a few more recent works on the topics we have covered:

H.B. Acton, *The Morals of Markets* (London, Longman, 1971).

A.V. Campbell, *Moral Dilemmas in Medicine* (Edinburgh, Churchill Livingstone, 2nd edn, 1975).

A.V. Campbell, *Medicine, Health and Justice* (Edinburgh, Churchill Livingstone, 1978).

Central Council for Education and Training in Social Work, *Values in Social Work*, CCETSW Paper 13 (London, CCETSW, 1976).

Antony Flew, *Crime or Disease?* (London, Macmillan, 1973).

Jonathan Glover, *Causing Death and Saving Lives* (Harmondsworth, Penguin, 1977).

R. Plant, *Social and Moral Theory in Casework* (London, Routledge & Kegan Paul, 1970).

Noel Timms and David Watson (eds), *Philosophy in Social Work* (London, Routledge & Kegan Paul, 1978).

Noel Timms (ed.), *Social Welfare: Why and How?* (London, Routledge & Kegan Paul, 1980).

Index